Where Has All the Power Gone?

Rev. Robert O. Faga

Order this book online at www.trafford.com
or email orders@trafford.com

Most Trafford titles are also available at major online book retailers.

Cover Illustration by David Ramey

Printed in the United States of America.

ISBN: 978-1-4669-7606-1 (sc)
ISBN: 978-1-4669-7605-4 (e)

Trafford rev. 02/13/2013

 www.trafford.com

North America & international
toll-free: 1 888 232 4444 (USA & Canada)
phone: 250 383 6864 ♦ fax: 812 355 4082

Dedicated to Sonnie Jean, my wife
since November 27, 1954

Contents

Foreword

THE CHURCH OF today is plagued by large backdoor losses and by slow gains in membership. This is true of most large denominations. While some of this can be attributed to the secularization of modern man's thinking, perhaps more of the problem can be found in some misunderstanding within the church.

The major concern of this book is the power of God as it works in individual lives and in the church. The question "Where has all the power gone?" is used as a comparison of the church today with the early church. The early church "turned the world upside down" while we manage to be satisfied with holding our own or at least be satisfied with a very small loss.

Church power comes from individual power. We cannot pray for the church to be strengthened without working for the individual to be strengthened. For the church to have power, members must be empowered from God.

We need the power of God in our lives. While many realize this, few know how to obtain it in the right way. Realizing a need for more power, some have advocated and practiced wrong means in obtaining it. This often leads to a fracturing of churches and friendships. However, there are proper means for Christians to increase the power of God in their lives. Using these means has a tendency to draw people closer to God and to one another.

We need power from God. We need it to stand firm in our faith against all adversity. We need power at times just to go on believing. Illness, death, business reverses, and poverty are only a few shocks our faith must withstand. Sin, searing the conscience and alienating friends, threatens to destroy the faith by which we call ourselves Christian. The devil seeks to destroy our faith through temptation, sin, and doubt. God has given us means whereby we can stand in the evil day.

We need the power of God in our lives not only for defense but also for offence. We, as Christians, have been told to do many things. We will do them only insofar as we have the power of God in our lives enabling us to do them. The physically weak cannot perform great physical feats. The spiritually weak do not perform great spiritual feats. This book seeks to show Christians where and how to obtain the power of God and so to become spiritually strong—enabled to stand and empowered to do.

This book asks those who are doing nothing to do something, and those who are doing something to do more, and those who are craving for greater spiritual events to harness their spiritual drive according to the proper channels of the Spirit's operation.

God gives saving faith. No one can lead himself to believe in Jesus, and no one can convert another; but once faith in Jesus is given by the Holy Spirit through the Gospel, there are things Christians can do and should do. This book deals with some of these things. The Bible says, "Work out your salvation with fear and trembling" (Phil.2:12). In another place, it is said, "Fight the good fight of faith . . ." (1 Timothy 6:12). These passages do not say we are saved by our own works or effort, but are simply saying that there are things we can and should do to strengthen the saving faith which the Lord has planted in our hearts. If the principles set forth in this book are practiced by an individual on a daily basis under the influence of the Holy Spirit, his faith will grow. As each of us grows weaker, the whole church is weakened. As each of us grows in faith, the whole church is strengthened. The church increases its own strength by strengthening its members. We contribute to the whole church by our own personal growth in Christ Jesus and His Word.

The primary concern of this book is the Lutheran Church and its membership although Christians of other denominations will find it of practical value. The Lutheran Church over the years has stood strong on the Scriptures and its Confessions. The emphasis of this book is not in changing this, but encouraging a greater involvement in practicing the principles we confess and believe—to practice what we preach. We will witness the power of God in our lives and in the life of the church as we move from a mouth and head affirmation to a heart and soul involvement.

It is not enough only to believe something as Jesus pointed out: "Whoever hears these sayings of Mine, and *does* them, I will liken him to a wise man who built his house on a rock" (italics mine) (New King James Version, Matt. 7:24).

The quotations from the Bible in this book are from the New American Standard Bible unless it is noted otherwise.

Rev. Robert O. Faga

Chapter 1

The Examination Room

THOUSANDS OF CHRISTIANS, including ministers and lay people, have compared the early Christian church to their present church and have asked, "Where has all the power gone?" They wish the present day church could be as dynamic as the church in its infancy. Unfortunately, there are too many people who think it is impossible for the church to be anything like it was, or they are satisfied with the church limping along in its weakened condition. They glory in what the church was and not in what it is today.

There are those who want to see a change and they teach how the early church was. "They were continually devoting themselves to the apostles' teaching and to fellowship, to the breaking of bread and to prayer" (Acts 2:42). "To be the church," it is taught, "we must teach what the apostles taught, have fellowship meetings in the church, celebrate Holy Communion, and pray." Even though these things are taught, the church, as a whole, never seems to come close to what it once was. Many have learned to accept conditions as they are. They stick doggedly to a routine established for them first by their grandparents and then by their parents. They say, "My Dad went to church every Sunday and therefore I go to church every Sunday." They are so persistent that they go through the motions no matter how painful it might be. They have developed the attitude, "As our fathers endured; so shall we." We say, "God bless them," for we do need perseverance in steadfastly holding to and doing what is right in the sight of God, but there is more.

People of God should expect great things. They should be expectant people saying, "What has God planned for today?" We should expect things to happen beyond the normal and the routine. God is involved, and our God is a God of miracles. He is the one, true, living God. We need to start asking the question "What difference is there between our meeting, whether in an organization or of a committee, and a meeting held by a group of atheists?" You may answer, "Well, we open our meeting and close our meeting with prayer." We should, however, be asking, "Where is God and His kingdom between those two prayers? Do we dismiss Him after the opening prayer and call Him back for the benediction?" The point is that a meeting of Christians should be dramatically different from a meeting of atheists.

Perhaps some of our deadness, our weary religious ways, have been part of our lives because of some faulty notions. You should be reminded of the fact that we are in the examination room where we are examining ourselves and being examined to determine why we do not have power. The promise of Jesus was "You shall receive power when the Holy Spirit has come upon you . . ." (Acts 1:8). Do you have that power? Have you experienced that power? If we the people or we the church do not have the power, we had better start asking, "Why not?" In this chapter, we will see some faulty notions we may have and throughout the book we will see other things that may very well be hindering the power of God in our midst.

First, we may have the attitude that religion is not supposed to be fun. Some people object to using the guitar in church for a youth service because their music makes us want to tap our feet and religion is a serious business. We would be foolish to consider dropping our formal services. Some churches have only informal services and so they have no option. Having formal services give to us the option, at least on occasion, to have informal services. However, there are some things a formal service does not mean. It does not mean that we cannot laugh in church if the minister happens to bring a joke into his sermon as an illustration. We can smile in church. We do not have to sit there drab-faced, as if waiting for an impending doom. Religion is a serious business, but it does not have to be drab and sorrowful. I write songs, and sometimes I wonder if the beat might be offensive to God, but as I think about it, I realize that it is not the beat that might be offensive but the attitude of the heart. A pastor friend of mine showed me a bulletin with a typographical error. It reads, "The children will be sinning beween the Epistle and Gospel readings." It may be true that the children were sinning while they were singing just like adults who sing with the voice and mind but not with the spirit and heart.

Secondly, we can miss out on the power because of another faulty notion. We have heard the expression "Might makes right." That is false, of course. Just because a man is the champion boxer of the world does not make his religion right. Can we turn this expression around and find one of our own problems? "Right makes might." With that we might be saying we have it all if we teach what is true. To teach the absolute truth is essential. "If the bugle produces an indistinct sound, who will prepare himself for battle?" (1 Cor. 14:8). It is, however, a faulty notion to assume that all we have to do is teach doctrine, and if people hear and learn doctrine, we will experience the power of God. To know the doctrine is not enough. It must be practiced. We cannot experience the power of God unless His commands are carried out and His promises are believed and acted upon. Because this has not been happening, we find churches of the living God dead serious and drab. We find this to be a problem for our Sunday schools, Christian day schools, and in the learning situations of our adult education. What is not used is lost seems to express what happens.

We have heard the illustration of the Dead Sea so often and yet we still do not get the message. Water flows into the Dead Sea but there is no outlet and as a result the water is stagnant and polluted. It is not living water. It must be obvious that we have filled our people with doctrine but have not provided them with proper outlets. So the power of God is not experienced. You may see a minister who is a happy, living saint, and you listen to him gladly; wishing in your heart you could be like him. You cannot have what he has just by listening to him. You must hear what he says, you must believe what he teaches, but you must also do what he does. It is, of course, easier to see the problem than it is to find the cure, but the people of God need to spend some overtime hours finding ways for every child of God to practice the precious truths that he believes. Jesus said, "Blessed are those who hear the word of God, and observe it" (Luke 11:28). And again, "Everyone who hears these words of Mine, and acts upon them, may be compared to a wise man, who built his house upon the rock" (Matt. 7:24).

Thirdly, we can be held back by a hidden oracle. God has not revealed it, preachers have not preached it, and teachers have not taught it, and yet many people seem to hold to it. In fact, when I was younger, I will admit, I held to it. The faulty dogma is this: "Everything my church teaches is right, therefore my church has everything." I am a Lutheran and I intend to be for the rest of my life. As a Lutheran, I believe, I have had things that people in other denominations have not had. One of the great blessings of the Lutheran Church is our educational system for teaching doctrinal truth. We have two or three year programs for the instruction of our young. We have Sunday schools and parochial schools, and also a mandatory instruction class for our new converts. Some churches have used this against us saying that if a prospect joins our church, he will have to go two or three months to our instruction classes, and then indicating that if they join their church, they will not have to go through this time-consuming procedure. Fortunately, this argument does not always work because there are many people who are hungering for spiritual knowledge, and others who prefer knowing what a church teaches before they join it. Every pastor will tell you that nearly 100 percent of the people who take the adult instruction classes, if not thrilled by them, are at least thankful for having had the opportunity. This is just one example of what I think is a particular blessing of God upon the Lutheran Church. We have other things which other denominations should examine with the possibility of including them in their program.

At the same time, as a Lutheran, I feel I have missed out on some things practiced in other denominations. Just because we believe that everything we have is right does not mean we have everything. Just because other denominations have what we may call false doctrine does not mean they have nothing. Perhaps we do not practice a Christian principle because we fear the label. We hear it said, for example, "That is Baptist, or that is Pentecostal, or that is Reformed," as if it could not be Lutheran. It is unfortunate for the church when it shuns a practice simply because it is used in another denomination. Having various distinct denominations is not as harmful to the Holy Christian Church as some people tend to think; but what is harmful is when a church will not practice a certain principle or work because another denomination is practicing the same thing.

We have been in the examining room and we have looked at a few things which perhaps have hindered the power of God in our lives and in the life of the church. While this book will not cover every obstacle, it will deal with some things we hear about but in actuality do not do.

Where has all the power gone? I do not know about you, but as for me, I want my religion to be more than just mechanical. Sure, I will do things simply because they are the right things to do; but we have been promised more than a mechanical and meaningless religion. We have been promised "peace" which is not of this world; we have been promised "joy" in the middle of trial and tribulation; and we have been promised power even in our weakest condition. I want that, don't you? We have seen the church discovering peace in the middle of persecution as they gathered together for prayer. We have seen the church finding joy in persecution as we see Paul and Silas singing in prison. We have seen the church experiencing power as they "upset the world" (Acts 17:6). I want that for our church today, don't you?

Oh, make Thy church, dear Savior,
A lamp of burnished gold
To bear before the nations
Thy true light as of old!
Oh, teach Thy wan-d'ring pilgrims
By this their path to trace
Till, clouds and darkness ended,
They see Thee face to face! TLH 294

Chapter 2

The Foundation

SOME YEARS AGO as a young man, I was asked the question "What does your church teach?" You may wish that a similar door for witnessing were opened to you. Since I blew it the first time, I have often hoped for another opportunity such as that. My friends and I were showing a visitor the inside of our church. This young man came out with the bold question, "What does your church teach?" It would be good if you would answer the question before you read on. The ball was tossed to me, and I fumbled it. Do you know what I said? I was really flustered, and blurted out, "Oh, our church teaches a lot of things." The whole catechism passed before my eyes. I was thinking of all the good I could do if we only had three or four days together. At least, I thought, he could be a little more specific. We left the church, climbed into the car, and even though we were on our way down the road, my mind was still back in the church. I was troubled because I had given no real answer to the man even though I loved my church very much. As I was thinking, it dawned on me what I should have said. So I awkwardly brought up the subject again saying, "You know the question you asked me about what our church teaches. Well, we believe that Jesus died for our sins on the cross." That was it. Better late than never, but as I think back, it was like throwing a log in the stove after the embers had died out. I never saw the young man before or ever after, and I still hope that God did use my late and feeble effort.

"What does your church teach?" I know that we have a doctrinal system which is very important to us, and each teaching is vital to our spiritual life in some way. Our doctrinal system is a "many splendored thing." There is, however, one source from which all doctrines gain their value; it is the person of Jesus Christ. What does your church teach? Our first answer should be "Jesus Christ—I believe that Jesus Christ lived, died, and rose again for my sins."

Jesus Christ is the most important part of the church. He is the foundation, and the only foundation, on which the church can build. "No man can lay a foundation other than the one which is laid, which is Jesus Christ" (1 Cor. 3:11). It is in Him where we, the people of the church, find answers to life's most important questions. Religion has significance for us only as we have a personal relationship with Him. It is the lack of the personal relationship which turns people off as far as the church is concerned; the reason why so many youth lose their religion, so to speak, when they go away to college. We need to see the turning away, the failure to do what is right, and the doing of what is wrong as all being symptoms of the same problem—no personal relationship with Jesus Christ.

The people of the world have many questions about religion, and we have answers in Jesus Christ. More and more, as we invite people to church, and as we witness to them, we find those who are agnostic. The most outstanding feature of an agnostic is his belief that even though there may be a god, no one can ever know Him in a personal way. Yet most people have a deep desire to know God. The cry of the human heart, often even in a Christian, is as we see in the book of Job, "Oh, that I knew where I might find him, that I might come even to his seat!" (Job 23:3). The hearts of thousands and millions of people are asking, "Where can I find God?" Suppose someone were to ask you that question, what would you say?

We can defend the existence of God by pointing to His creation or to our own conscience which tells us that there is a higher law than our own. He will be much more effective if we point to Jesus Christ. Very seldom do people question the reality of Jesus Christ. Generally, people think of Him as the most important person who ever lived. When people ask the question "Where can I find God?" we need to point to the manger-crib, for this baby was "God manifested in the flesh" (1 Tim. 3:16). "God was in Christ reconciling the world to Himself . . ." (2 Cor. 5:19). "In the beginning was the Word, and the Word was with God, and the Word was God. He was in the beginning with God" (John 1:1-2). "And the Word became flesh, and dwelt among us, and we saw His glory, glory as of the only begotten from the Father, full of grace and truth" (John 1:14).

A stimulating question is "Who appears more friendly to you, God or Jesus?" Most people will answer, "Jesus." It is really not a fair question, but in asking it, we can lead people to understand that God is as friendly and loving as Jesus because Jesus is God. When Jesus was in the world, the religious leaders were opposed to Him. On the other hand, the common people heard Him gladly. They flocked to Him from everywhere because He had compassion on them—He pitied them—He loved them. He healed their sicknesses, forgave their sins, prayed for them, and wept for them. They knew He loved them. That is what God is like because Jesus is God. When people are troubled with the problem of finding God, we can tell them, "Go to Jesus, and you will know God and what He is like."

It is not enough to know that Jesus was the greatest man who ever lived, or that His teachings were the greatest ever taught, or that He was the most loving person who ever lived. Many false conclusions can come from knowing this and no more. There is another question that troubles mankind. It is: "How can man be in the right before God?" (Job 9:2). or "How can he be clean who is born of woman?" (Job 25:4). For a question like these, we simply point to the cross. Man's basic problem is sin. Men have tried about everything in dealing with this problem. They have tried to bribe God with their money. They have tried to appease God with their works, offerings, and sacrifices.

They have tried to obtain God's pity by torturing their bodies. But sin remains sin, and it sticks to a man like a shadow. You cannot push a shadow away, explain it away, or run away from it. It is just there, and so it is with sin. The Bible describes the whole human race when it says, "All of us have become like one who is unclean, and all our righteous deeds are like a filthy garment . . ." (Is. 64:6).

The cross, in reality, is the altar on which Jesus offered the greatest sacrifice. God placed our sins upon Jesus and punished Him in our stead. "The Lord was pleased to crush Him, putting Him to grief . . ." (Is. 53:10). He was "stricken, smitten of God, and afflicted" (Is. 53:4). By this one act of Jesus Christ upon the cross, the whole world was declared righteous in the sight of God. This is the heart of our teaching; "God so loved the world, that He gave His only begotten Son, that whoever believes in Him should not perish, but have eternal life" (John 3:16). How can man be justified before God? The answer is the cross and the death of Jesus Christ and nothing else.

There is one more question that is troublesome to man. It is: "If a man dies, will he live again?" (Job 14:14). Again, we point to Jesus Christ and this time to the empty tomb. Death is a troubling thought for most people. We will all die—it is inevitable. People think of death often; some think about it every day. With every passing day, we know we are one day closer to our own death. The hope for a Christian is in the fact that Jesus Christ who died on the cross rose again from the dead. If it were not for the resurrection of Jesus Christ, our religion would be nothing. We would have nothing for ourselves or for anyone else. As one man said, "Let us admit that if they should find the body of Jesus, our religion is nothing." Paul wrote it in his letter to the Corinthians: "If Christ has not been raised, your faith is worthless; you are still in your sins" (1 Cor. 15:17). It can be an exciting experience for Christians to read *Evidence That Demands A Verdict* by Josh McDowell. He goes to great lengths to show the one logical explanation for the missing body. It was true as the angel said, "He is not here, but He has risen . . ." (Luke 24:6). Our hope to live after this life is based on what Jesus has already done. He said, "Because I live, you will live also."(John 14:19)

It is as we place this emphasis on Jesus Christ that our religion takes on meaning and strength. No other religion can offer as much as Christians do with the same confidence. No one can explode our religion as someone would pop a balloon because our faith is based on the solid rock—the person of Jesus Christ. It is important that we hold to and point to the historical reality of Jesus.

Christianity is not one religion among many. It is the one, true religion of the creator God. On one occasion, I had the opportunity to speak to a woman, who along with her husband, was involved in the study of the Eastern religions. I ignored what I knew about her so I could have an opportunity to present the Gospel. After I had made my presentation, I asked her if she would like to invite Christ into her life. Her answer was, "You sound sincere in what you believe, but I can find people in all these other religions who are just as sincere as you are." I answered her as calmly as I could, "This may be true, but it doesn't really matter what I might think, or what you might think, or what anyone else might think. What is important is how things really are. One must not only live by what he believes; but he must also die by what he believes; and I don't know of any other person, other than Jesus Christ, who has lived, died and rose again for my sins."

We must, however, go beyond history and facts. In the present, we need a personal relationship with Jesus Christ. We must accept Him as our Savior. If we have already done this, we should let Him know that He is welcome in our lives every hour of every day. Jesus said, "I am the vine, you are the branches; he who abides in Me, and I in him, he bears much fruit, for apart from Me you can do nothing" (John 15:5). It is not enough for us to have received Christ once in our life. Daily, we must believe in Him. We must trust in Him for forgiveness and for salvation which He has earned for us on the cross and which He verified by His resurrection from the dead.

It would be good if outsiders could look at our church and say, "They teach Jesus Christ." As a church, we can become known for a negative stand rather than for a positive witness. The stand we take is important. We do not benefit ourselves or anyone else by ignoring unpopular Biblical teaching. What others know about our church is also important. It happens too often where a church in a community is known as the church which is "opposed to this and opposed to that." I have talked to many members who express a weariness over having to defend a position which they themselves have difficulty understanding. It can be different. A man explained one of my visits this way, "When others came to visit us, they explained how their church was organized and showed slides of church buildings; but when he came, he talked about Jesus Christ, and I couldn't get him off the subject." It should always be this way. We should be known as people who teach and preach about Jesus Christ. He is the foundation for everything else that we believe and teach.

A church can be associated with Jesus. The Ongoing Ambassadors for Christ visited our church for a weekend. As is their usual custom, they witnessed about Christ in our community. Shortly after that, the Evangelists made calls on some of the prospects found by the youth. It was enough for one person to comment after our second visit, "The Jesus' freaks were down to see us again." When I first heard it, I said, "Praise the Lord!" For even though this was a sarcastic remark, the person knew what our main message was. "The church's one foundation is Jesus Christ her Lord."

Where has all the power gone? Perhaps we need to ask, "What is central in our teaching?" We may feel that the main issues of today are such things as abortion, capital punishment, pollution, or communism. While we need to speak out on present issues, there is one issue which must stand first and above all the rest; that a person consider the claims of Jesus Christ. Paul and Peter spoke about Jesus as the Christ, whom men crucified, and whom God raised from the dead. "Philip went down to the city of Samaria and began proclaiming Christ to them"

(Acts 8:5). When he was in the chariot with the Ethiopian Eunuch, "Philip opened his mouth, and beginning from this Scripture he preached Jesus to him" (Acts 8:35). In Achaia, it is said that Apollos was "demonstrating by the Scriptures that Jesus was the Christ" (Acts 18:28). For this reason, the church experienced power. Every time they opened their mouths, Jesus came out.

What does your church teach? The more central Jesus becomes in our thinking, preaching, and teaching, the more we will experience the power of His personal presence.

The Church's one foundation Is Jesus Christ, her Lord; She is His new creation By water and the Word. From heav'n He came and sought her To be His holy Bride; With His own blood He bought her, And for her life He died.

TLH—473

Chapter 3

In Sackcloth and Ashes

RELIGION IS NOT all joy and happy times. There are times when hymns need to be sung in a minor key and times when tears flow down our cheeks. We need to see our sins in the light of the cross as we sing, "Ye who think of sin but lightly Nor suppose the evil great Here may view its nature rightly, Here its guilt may estimate" (TLH 153). We must have this serious contemplation because we need repentance. As we go through these unhappy moments of taking a good look at our dreadful deeds, we can be assured of the fact that after the cloudy day, the sun is going to be shining much more brightly. Among the first words Jesus spoke in his public ministry, He said, "Repent and believe the Gospel" (Mark 1:15).

The Bible makes it clear that we are saved by faith alone in Jesus Christ. Faith in its simplest form can be described as a desire for Jesus to save. The thief on the cross said, "Remember me when You come into Your kingdom!"(Luke 23:42). His faith was alive as he placed his only hope for heaven into the hands of Jesus. On the other hand, it is not true as some say, "It does not really matter what you do. What is important is believing." I do not save myself by refraining from sin and by doing good. We know Jesus earned forgiveness and eternal life for us by His death and resurrection. What He has earned is given as a gift to us who believe. Yet we can say, "It does matter what you do."

I don't know any Christian who would say, "Sin is good for you." Rather, we believe sin hurts people; it is sin that destroys everything that is bright and beautiful. Sin can destroy faith. While I do not want to get into the issue of which sins destroy faith, or the time when faith is destroyed, we must see the harmful nature of sin. For our purpose, let us say, "All sin is destructive of faith, and some sins more than others," with the thinking in mind that a wind may be destructive without destroying the house. Because sin is destructive, we examine ourselves according to the ten commandments. Everyone sins. King Solomon included this in his dedication prayer, "For there is no person who does not sin . . ." (2 Chron. 6:36). So everyone needs repentance. It sounds too simple to expect a problem in this area of our spiritual life. However, a problem exists for us to the extent that we are not aware of our sins. Sin is harmful to faith whether we are aware of a sin or not.

A new convert to the faith said that he continued to sleep with his girlfriend after his conversion because he did not know it was wrong. After he learned it was wrong, he changed the situation by getting married. We need to see what is wrong with our lives by reading the law. We will know what is wrong, we will see the need of repentance, if we read the following Scripture passages prayerfully. As you read, ask the Holy Spirit to open your eyes to see the sin or sins that are harmful to you. "Do you not know that the unrighteous will not inherit the kingdom of God? Do not be deceived; neither fornicators, nor idolaters, nor adulterers, nor effeminate, nor homosexuals, nor thieves, nor the covetous, nor drunkards, nor revilers, nor swindlers, shall inherit the kingdom of God" (1 Cor. 6:9-10). The first president of the Lutheran Church-Missouri Synod said of the above passage, "The Christian's repentance consists in this, that he desires to commit these sins no more."1 We read similar words in Galatians, "Now the deeds of the flesh are evident, which are: immorality, impurity, sensuality, idolatry, sorcery, enmities, strife, jealousy, outbursts of anger, disputes, dissensions, factions, envying, drunkenness, carousing, and things like these, of which I forewarn you, just as I have forewarned you, that those who practice such things will not inherit the kingdom of God" (Gal. 5:19-21).

Surely after we have read these passages, we can see some of our own sins, perhaps even grievous sins. These sins can send us to hell unless we repent.

A Christian still sins every day even though he does not want to. An illustration might prove helpful. Picture a bucket filled with water, and let the water represent faith. Sins can be likened to holes in the bucket which allow the water to drain away. Since some sins are bigger than others, the holes in the bucket would vary. Telling a white lie would not be as destructive of faith as committing adultery. Let us see what can be done about the drain on our faith. For example, from the list of sins in the Bible passages above, think about one, "outbursts of anger." Suppose you are sitting in your chair reading the evening newspaper, and your child comes to talk to you. At first you might calmly tell him not to bother you, but if he persists, you might become angry and shout, "Didn't I tell you that I don't want to be bothered now?" The child may have done nothing wrong except wanting to speak to you. You sinned by your angry outburst and needed to repent. At that moment, you should have prayed, "Lord, I am sorry that I became angry with my child. Please forgive me for Jesus' sake." It is better to tell the child also admitting you were wrong. Following the above illustration, a hole was put in the bucket which caused a drain on faith; but when there was sorrow and a need for forgiveness, God would readily forgive and the drain on our faith would be stopped. All of our sins need to be dealt with in this way. Our deeds must be seen as sin, confessed, repented of, and God's forgiveness accepted through Jesus Christ.

It is easier to see the sins of others than it is to see our own. There is a reason for this. Suppose someone becomes angry at you, and with some very loud and strong language puts you down. You recognize what he did as sin because you were hurt by it. When we do the same thing to someone else, we do not recognize it as sin because we feel justified in doing it. We can always find a reason for our own actions.

Some sins are more readily recognized than others. They are not only recognized by others, but also by those who are guilty of doing them. Quick condemnation comes upon those who are guilty of adultery, murder, and theft. The offending party is aware of his sin because of public condemnation. They know they have sinned. Others make them know it. This perhaps is the main reason Jesus said, "The tax collectors and prostitutes will get into the kingdom of God before you" (Matt. 21:31). Other sins do not seem as severe because we do not have much public accusation against them. The first four commandments seem to carry little force today. They are often broken with little serious thought. Yet not only were adulterers and murderers stoned in the Old Testament; but also capital punishment was in order for those who were guilty of breaking the first four commandments. We need to see idolatry, cursing with God's name, not attending church, disobeying and dishonoring parents as serious violations of God's holy law. All the sins mentioned are damaging to us.

However, the most dangerous sins for the average Christian may not be any of these. The sins of our hearts may be even more damaging for there is nothing outside of ourselves to warn us about them. To make matters worse, according to psychology, a person has no idea what he is really like. He is the worst judge of his own character. Because of this, many people in the church are able to avoid having their self-righteous character punctured. This evasion is harmful to the health of any church and of any individual. There is only one way we can know our sinful condition. This is through the light from the Holy Spirit shining on the Scriptures and in our hearts—to pray for such enlightenment is an aid to spiritual health.

Perhaps we do not see the power of God in the church today because we do not feel a need for much forgiveness. Jesus told a Pharisee, "He who is forgiven little, loves little" (Luke 7:47). He was talking about Pharisees. They were just the opposite of the sinful woman who was washing his feet with her tears and wiping them with her hair. She knew her sins were great and truly appreciated the forgiveness which

Jesus stood for and gave to her. The Pharisee, whose sins, no doubt, were as great as hers or greater, was not aware of his sin, thought he needed little or no forgiveness, and as a result loved only a little if at all. Can it be that the church is not experiencing the power of God because there are too many sins in the lives of our people that are covered and hidden; or if uncovered, not confessed and repented of? Pharisees cannot experience the power of God because they trust in their own power and work righteousness and not in the power of the blood of Christ.

Do we really mean what we say, "I, a poor miserable sinner, confess unto Thee?" Can we really say and mean it: "God be merciful to me a sinner"? Sometimes I wonder if St. Paul would feel a little uncomfortable to say in our circles, "Christ Jesus came into the world to save sinners, of whom I am chief" (1 Tim.1:15). Would people say, "What great evil has he done?" and ever after look at Paul and wonder what it was that made him so sinful. In reality, it was Paul's good fortune to have seen the X-rays of himself taken by the Holy Spirit through the law. He saw his condition clearly as he said, "The good that I want, I do not do, but I practice the very evil that I do not want. Wretched man that I am! Who will set me free from the body of this death?" (Rom. 7:19, 24). Paul had no hope in himself; but he did have hope as he said, "Thanks be to God, who gives us the victory through our Lord Jesus Christ" (1 Cor. 15:57).

A president of the United States shocked some people, and was ridiculed by some, when he admitted having had lust in his heart for other women. Generally, church people do not want others to know of the hidden vices they have. We can feel very uncomfortable when someone tells us that he has this lust in his heart. It is much easier for all to say together, "Oh, yes, we all do." It is more difficult for us to admit, "I have had lust in my heart for a person who is not my spouse." It is difficult because we are afraid the other person has not had lust, or else he would not admit it. We do not want to appear more sinful than our peers. But we are backed up by the Bible, by a countless number of saints of God, testifying to the fact that in every human heart, including the hearts of our saintly older women, there is lust, envy, hatred, and covetousness. Jeremiah was God's spokesman as he wrote, "The heart is more deceitful than all else and is desperately sick; who can understand it? I, the Lord, search the heart, I test the mind, even to give to each man according to his ways, according to the results of his deeds" (Jer.17:9-10). The beauty of a person does not consist of outward appearance; but in the dealing with the inward problem of sinful desire.

An awareness of sin without faith leads to despair; but faith without the present awareness of sin can lead to self-righteousness. The Pharisees were people who were concerned about the outside of the cup, and as a result, they could appear as good men to those around them. Because others looked upon them as good, they felt even more justified by what they did. They were able to keep all their secret sins hidden from view. To keep us from being Pharisees, to be aware of our sinful condition, we need to pray with the Psalmist, "Search me, O God, and know my heart; try me and know my anxious thoughts; and see if there be any hurtful way in me, and lead me in the everlasting way" (Psalm 139:23-24).

Some people are unwilling to admit that what they are doing is sin. They justify their feeling or action rather than confessing it, and are harmed tremendously by it. I visited a home of an elderly couple who had deep, bitter feelings toward a pastor who had refused to have a funeral service for their son. As I listened, I could see how miserable they were as this bitterness ate away at them. After they had finished talking, I said, "I do not know whether the pastor was right or wrong, for I am not in a position to judge. The pastor is an individual who also must act according to his conscience. If he was wrong, he would have to answer to God for it." Then I showed them how this act of the pastor had led them to hate, to be bitter, to slander him often, and in doing this, they were sinning against God. Even though the pastor may have provoked their action, they were still responsible to God for the sins of their own hearts and tongues. The sin was actually hurting them more than the person they wanted to harm.

I have witnessed congregations torn apart because of some incident in the past. People were not talking to each other. They were sitting on the opposite side of the church. They were not communing together. These were all evidences of an unforgiving heart. No doubt, both parties felt justified in their ostracism of the other, but the painful truth is that spiritual growth is smothered as long as bitterness, anger, and hatred remain. When will we ever learn? We are told, "Never take your own revenge . . . Vengeance is Mine, I will repay, says the Lord" (Rom. 12:19). According to these passages, we are guilty of disobedience and doubt when we try to get even. We are disobedient because the Lord has told us not to get revenge. We are guilty of doubt because we do not believe God will bring justice into the situation. Whether a person is right or wrong in hurting you, you hurt yourself by maintaining a vengeful attitude. It is a sin that is destructive of faith. We have been taught by the Lord in His Word, "Do not be overcome by evil, but overcome evil with good" (Rom. 12:21). The sins of others must not lead us to retaliate with sins of our own. We must learn how to meet unkindness with love and forgiveness, and to recognize it as sin when we do not.

Repentance is necessary, and not to repent of any known sin is very destructive of faith. Repentance means sorrow for having sinned against a loving God. It is not a sorrow for getting caught or for the consequences of sin that one might suffer. Repentance means turning away from sin whether or not we feel like it. We are to turn from sin to God who forgives us. While our feelings about sin may not be changed for some time, forgiveness comes at the moment of confession. This is important because feelings must not be associated with forgiveness. "How do we know if we are truly sorry for our sins?" I was once asked. God does not expect us to change our feelings about sin; it is a work He alone can do. He does expect us to confess it, to acknowledge it, and to call sin by its right name, sin. Outwardly we are to turn from sin; but only God can turn us inwardly. For every sin, there must be the cycle of confession, repentance, and trust in the Lord Jesus Christ for forgiveness. We may have to go through this procedure a dozen or more times for a particular sin in our life. The Bible calls it "The sin which so easily entangles us" (Heb. 12:1). Only as we see all Jesus endured for us, only as we receive God's daily forgiveness, will we be given power to turn wholeheartedly from any known sin.

Repentance makes a different person out of you. Let us see what it means that "no adulterer, no murderer, etc." shall enter the kingdom of God. Suppose two men are guilty of murder, killing another person in cold blood. They both die; but as they stand before the judgment seat of God, one is guilty of murder and the other is not. One gets to go to heaven, but the other does not. One is a murderer and the other is not. What is the difference? The difference is not to be found in the motive for killing. It is found in repentance. One man is a murderer as he stands before God, because he was not sorry for his sin. He did not trust in Jesus for forgiveness. The other man was not a murderer because he was sorry for his sin, and he believed that "The blood of Jesus His (God's) Son cleanses us from all sin" (1 John 1:7). Repentance makes a different person out of you. A repentant murderer is no longer considered a murderer in the sight of God.

When we are aware of the destructive nature of sin, there should not be any sin that we would want to hang on to. If I think of my sin as holding back the power of God, or that bitterness in me is hurting my life and my relationship with others, or that an unforgiving attitude has taken hold of me to my harm, why should I want to keep it? Jesus was speaking about a calamity that happened and was asking people if they thought the disaster victims were guilty of some great sin. Then He said, "I tell you, no, but unless you repent, you will all likewise perish" (Luke 13:3). Why should I not repent? Why should I let even the sins of others do damage to me, to my character, and above all, to my relationship with God?

To experience the power of God's love and forgiveness, we need to repent. A few years ago, I read a beautiful prayer of repentance in one of the *Day by Day with Jesus* devotions. I have had it in my Bible ever since. Based on and including Lamentations 5:21, it reads like this: "Turn Thou us unto Thee, O Lord, and we shall be turned! Turn me from sin, from hell, from eternal death! Turn me from my own sinful flesh, from my own lustful thoughts, my own selfish, hateful, revengeful self! Turn me from the lure and lust of temptation! Turn me from the despair over my transgressions, from the accusation of my conscience, from the fear of death! Turn me from Thy wrath, and for Jesus' sake bring me into Thy love!" We need a repentant prayer like this.

Where has all the power gone? Sin is destructive when God's love and forgiveness are not experienced. As a result there is a loss of power in our lives. It is simply drained away. We need those times when we wear sackcloth and ashes, for then we will be prepared to experience the riches of God's forgiveness given to us through His Son. This repentance comes easier for us as we shall see in the next chapter. The Holy Spirit points through the gloom of our sin to the cross where alone we can find reconciliation with our God.

Lord, to Thee I make confession; I have sinned and gone astray, I have multiplied transgression, Chosen for myself my way. Led by Thee to see my errors, Lord, I tremble at Thy terrors.

> Then on Him I cast my burden,
> Sink it in the depths below.
> Let me know Thy gracious pardon,
> Wash me, make me white as snow.
> Let Thy Spirit leave me never;
> Make me only Thine forever. TLH 326

1. Law and Gospel, Dr. C.F.W. Walther, page 320

Chapter 4

In a Garment as White as Snow

IN THE APOSTLES' Creed, we confess, "I believe in . . . the forgiveness of sins." In other words, we believe there is such a thing as a blotting out of all sin or an erasing of all sins marked against us. Forgiveness means having a clean slate before God. Unfortunately, many people in our churches today do not seem to find peace and joy from this good news. They find peace and joy in the wrong things or in the wrong ways. So they have a peace which can be disturbed and a joy which is not that fulfilling.

We have peace with God because God forgives. We have joy because our sins are not laid to our charge. David wrote in his Psalm, "How blessed is he whose transgression is forgiven, whose sin is covered! How blessed is the man to whom the Lord does not impute iniquity . . ." (Psalm 32:1-2). God's forgiveness means that He does not charge our sins to our account. So a person is blessed, or "happy" as some translations put it, when he can see no sin between him and his God. According to the above passage, we should be able to be happy every day. Failure to appropriate God's forgiveness is the main reason we have so much gloom in our lives and experience so little power in the church. Every day should be a "happy" day. Why? Because God forgives.

What we need is to wear the garment provided for us by God. There are enough "holy garments" for all the people of the world; and yet most people are still running around in their religious underwear; the rags of their own righteousness. Jesus told the parable of the great wedding feast. The invitations were sent out which said, "Behold, I have prepared my dinner . . . everything is ready; come to the wedding" (Matt. 22:4). The first invitations were ignored; but they continued to invite people until the wedding hall was filled with guests. When the king came in, he found a man who did not have on a wedding garment, and he said to him, "Friend, how did you come in here without wedding clothes?" We are told, "He was speechless" (Matt. 22:12). He had no excuse for not wearing a wedding garment since they were provided for all the guests.

There are people today who are speechless when they are asked about their soul's salvation. The parable teaches that even among Christians some are found who are not wearing the garment of forgiveness provided for them by God. The Bible is intended to lead us to believe that God has provided a garment as white as snow for every person in the world. John the Baptist described Jesus as "The Lamb of God who takes away the sin of the world" (John 1:29). The Bible tells about the perfectness of the attire God has provided for us. One such passage is found in Isaiah: "Come now, and let us reason together, says the Lord, though your sins are as scarlet, they will be as white as snow; though they are red like crimson, they will be like wool" (Is. 1:18). Jesus paid for the garment by His suffering and death; by shedding His blood upon the cross. By His sacrifice, He provided complete coverage for everyone. It is not a hundred dollar deductible policy, or a fifty, or even a 1¢ deductible. Jesus paid the entire cost so that those who trust in Him receive full coverage. We cannot pay anything, do anything, or even think we must do something for the coverage without losing it. We must simply believe we have it. Jesus offers everyone the forgiveness of sins and eternal life on the basis of what He did for them on the cross. We must see this as the "garment" purchased for us by Christ; a gift from God through His Son.

The word "garment" is being used as a symbolic word to represent God's total arid complete forgiveness of every person's sin. When it is said that there is a garment for everyone, it means that there is forgiveness for everyone. This good news of the Gospel gives us the ability to say to anyone and everyone, "Your sins are forgiven because Jesus has paid the price for them." To believe in Jesus is nothing else than believing your sins are forgiven because of what He had done on the cross and by His resurrection from the dead. When Jesus said on the cross, "My God, My God, why hast Thou forsaken Me?" (Matt. 27:46), He was suffering the torments of the damned in hell. On the cross, He was the worst sinner who ever lived because He had taken the sins of every person on Himself to pay the penalty for them. He had taken on Himself great sins and small sins, in fact, all sins—the sins of the prostitute, the thief, the liar, the homosexual, and the murderer. He paid in full the sin debt of every man—the sins of his past, present, and future. Faith is important because it is believing what God says about the death and resurrection of His Son. "He who was delivered up because of our transgressions, and was raised because of our justification" (Romans 4:25). Great things are now attributed to faith, and this means faith in Jesus. "He who believes in Him is not judged; he who does not believe has been judged already, because he has not believed in the name of the only begotten Son of God" (John 3:18). This was the witness of the early church: "Every one who believes in Him has received forgiveness of sins" (Acts 10:43). Jesus said it clearly: "He who believes has eternal life." It is as I wrote in one song:

> "Come to Me," the Savior said.
> "There's no other place to go;
> And though your sins are crimson red,
> They shall be as white as the snow."

This is what we must believe because it is true. "The Spirit and the bride say, 'Come.' And let the one who hears say, 'Come.' And let the one who is thirsty come; let the one who wishes take the water of life without cost" (Rev. 22:17). "Jesus said to them, 'I am the bread of life; he who comes to Me will not hunger, and he who believes in Me shall never thirst.'" (John 6:35). We should believe on the basis of these words. Yet there are obstacles or clouds that keep us from seeing things as they really are. The good news always sounds too good to be true, so let us look at some of the problems which keep people from believing in God's forgiveness. While we cannot hope to name all the problems, we should at least try to remove some of the stumbling blocks which keep people from wearing the "garment as white as snow."

While much has been written about the problem of work-righteousness, it is still one of the big reasons why people do not experience joy and peace through God's forgiveness. Work-righteousness is a part of our natural makeup. It means the effort a man puts forth to make himself holy by his good works—trying to provide himself with a garment to wear on judgment day. The Bible clearly tells us otherwise: "He saved us, not on the basis of deeds which we have done in righteousness, but according to His mercy . . ." (Titus 3:5). We can read in Paul's letter to the Ephesians that salvation is "not of yourselves . . . not as a result of works, so that no one may boast" (Eph. 2:8-9).

Rather than us earning heaven as if it is a reward for our good works, eternal life is a gift of God. "By grace you have been saved through faith . . . it is a gift of God . . ." (Eph. 2:8-9). Since it is a gift, it is free to all who will accept it. "The free gift of God is eternal life in Christ Jesus our Lord" (Rom. 6:23). We may confess that we are saved by grace but we hold a double standard when we think our works have something to do with saving us. Listen to what St. Paul wrote: "If it is by grace, it is no longer on the basis of works, otherwise grace is no longer grace" (Rom. 11:6). Grace means heaven is free; undeserved and unmerited. We need to exclude the thought of good works contributing to our forgiveness or to our obtaining heaven. To help exclude this from our thinking, we need to see the problems people face when they believe their works save them either completely or partially. When people think of their good deeds as in any way contributing to their salvation, they must still deal with the problem of sin. Very few people claim to be perfect. Most can be led to see their guilt because they have broken the rules they try to live by. What most do not understand is that you do not make up for a mistake by doing a good deed or two. For example, if you are driving your car and run a stop sign, and in the process hit another car, will the damage be undone if you stop at the sign every time thereafter? No, the deed is done. It is a mark against you. Sin means that you have not lived as you were supposed to live, and when you do a good deed, you are only doing what you should be doing anyway. So the good deed or deeds, no matter how many or what kind, never make up for the wrong we do. Our sin debt only grows larger with the passing of time. If our sin is great at age twenty-two, it will be greater at age twenty-three. There is even more to consider. Even the good deeds we do are imperfect. Isaiah said, "All of us have become like one who is unclean, and all our righteous deeds are like a filthy garment . . ." (Is. 64:6). If a person tries by his good deeds to provide his own garment to wear on judgment day, he will end up wearing a filthy garment—not one "as white as snow."

We need to admit our sinful condition and our utter helplessness. Some religions operate on the principle: "We are sinful because we sin." There is truth in this but it can lead to the idea that we become sinless when we stop sinning. The Biblical principle is better stated: "We sin because we are sinful." We must start with the basic premise that we are sinful by nature. It will explain why we sin but also it will make us realize that any hope of getting to heaven by works is hopeless. We are sinful by nature and we add to our sinfulness by our sinning. We pray a prayer nearly every Sunday morning in which we confess that "we are by nature, sinful and unclean—and that we have sinned against God by thought, word and deed." If a person believes he is saved by works, he must still come to grips with his sin and his sinful condition.

There must be forgiveness or there is no hope for any of us. Jesus said, "Unless your righteousness surpasses that of the scribes and Pharisees, you will not enter the kingdom of heaven" (Matt. 5:20). No one of that day would have said that the Pharisees never did good works. They fasted, they prayed, and they tithed. Jesus often pointed out the problems they had. However, He never said they did not do good works for they followed a code of ethics much of which was based on Old Testament Law. St. Paul said he "lived as a Pharisee according to the strictest sect of our religion" (Acts 26:5). So according to the above passage, if we plan to get to heaven by the works we do, we will have to be better than the best man who ever lived. Forgiveness is the only way we can be better than the best.

Those who believe they are saved by their works have an even greater problem to deal with. If we are to get to heaven by works, we have to be absolutely perfect. Jesus said, "You are to be perfect, as your heavenly Father is perfect" (Matt. 5:48). James, our Lord's brother, wrote: "Whoever keeps the whole law and yet stumbles in one point, he has become guilty of all" (James 2:10). We should believe this because the Bible says so. But let us look at it from a logical point of view. If we were to be saved by our works, what would God's standard be for letting us into heaven? If we say perfection, we can immediately see that no one would be in heaven. If we say anything less than perfection, we have to deal with another problem. What will the standard be? Some people believe that God will grade on a curve. They mean by this that the better ones will get to go to heaven. In doing this, they are using a form of logic. Since no one can be perfect, they reason, and since some people will surely be in heaven, God must have a lower standard to let some in. But where would the standard be set? If you get good points for being good and bad points for being bad, would it mean you have to do more good than bad in order to go to heaven? But if God had set a standard of 75 percent in order to pass, would it be fair for one who had 74 percent and flunked while another with 76 percent passed? Or would it be fair at all if God has set a standard such as 75 percent and never told anyone? But God has set the standard, and the standard is perfection. Man who trusts in his own good works will always fall short. He cannot provide a "garment" for himself suitable to wear on judgment day. We should want God's garment, the one we pray for as communicants: "Take off from them the spotted garment of their own righteousness and adorn them with the righteousness purchased by Thy blood." You will not accept God's forgiveness until you see it as absolutely necessary and until you see it as the only way for anyone.

Many will put too much emphasis on feelings. They say, "But I don't feel forgiven." There are things that keep us from feeling forgiven. It may be the consequences people suffer because of a sin they committed. A young girl may become pregnant outside of marriage. The pastor may speak to her of God's love and forgiveness, but she dos not feel forgiven because she is still pregnant and has to face her family, friends, and the people of the church. Such a person must see the "feelings" as being connected with the consequences rather than with the sin itself. The consequences of sin do not indicate that God does not love or forgive her. Forgiveness from God must be accepted by faith in Jesus. If she believes that God forgives her, accepts her as she is, then she must be led to believe that God is on her side to help, strengthen, and assist her in facing the consequences. If this is understood, she may experience a "good feeling" realizing that when no one else seems to care, God really cares about her.

Feelings should not be based upon a subjective experience as some would say, "I felt so close to God." Sometimes we may not feel close to God and can still believe we are forgiven. Feelings should be based on the objective reality of Jesus' death and resurrection. No matter how wrong things may go in life, you can always go to the cross of Christ and find assurance of God's love and forgiveness. From the event of the cross, you can affirm that God loves and cares for you more than anyone else in this world who loves or cares for you. Think of the words of God which were spoken through Isaiah: "Can a woman forget her nursing child, And have no compassion on the son of her womb? Even these may forget, but I will not forget you" (Is. 49:15). Good feelings come from knowing and believing that God loves you and forgives you for Jesus' sake. Faith is believing what God says to you in His Word in spite of what you hear, feel, or experience in the world.

Since people are the church, we must say that the church has not always done a good job in helping people to accept the forgiveness intended for them by God. Sometimes people find it difficult to accept forgiveness from God because the church does not know what to do if a fellow member falls into sin. Jesus knew how to deal with sinners, why don't we? We must, in some cases, believe an important thought. God is much more loving, kind, and forgiving than any of us will ever be. Think of this beautiful passage: "Seek the Lord while He may be found; Call upon Him while He is near. Let the wicked forsake his way, and the unrighteous man his thoughts; and let him return to the Lord, and He will have compassion on him, and to our God, for He will abundantly pardon. 'For My thoughts are not your thoughts, nor are your ways My ways,' declares the Lord, 'for as the heavens are higher than the earth, so are My ways higher than your ways, and My thoughts than your thoughts'" (Is. 55:6-9). When someone sins, it is often difficult for fellow church members to forgive him even after repentance; especially if the sin is committed more than once. The sinner can be made to feel unforgiven because of how he is treated by his fellow members. We need to see the loving heart of God shown to us by His Son. Jesus said, "Be on your guard! If your brother sins, rebuke him; and if he repents, forgive him. And if he sins against you seven times a day, and returns to you seven times, saying, 'I repent', forgive him" (Luke 17:3-4). Most Christians are excellent at rebuking the sinner; but we have much to learn about forgiveness. When a person feels rejected by the church, he may have to be reminded that our ways are so often not like God's. What the church teaches officially is not always practiced publicly by its members.

So the church should not be looked upon as an exact duplicate of God. Certainly, in confession and absolution, it stands in the place of Christ and the absolution must be received as coming from Christ Himself. I am speaking of the attitude of people so often displayed, and of the church which is often frail and weak and has made mistakes as seen from history. In the case of Judas, the church did not practice its function as it should have. Judas had committed the terrible sin of betraying his Lord. After the act, he came to his senses and realized what he had done. He came into the temple of God and made a beautiful confession of sin. He said, "I have sinned by betraying innocent blood . . . ." (Matt. 27:4). What should have been said was what Nathan the prophet said to David, "The Lord also has taken away your sin . . ." (2 Sam. 12:13). Instead, the priests said to Judas, "What is that to us? See to that yourself." (Matt. 27:4). Result: Judas "went away and hanged himself." This is one example of what an unforgiving church or unforgiving people can do.

History also tells of the time when an offender had to pass through stages to return to his regular church fellowship.1 For a year the offender lay prostrate and weeping in the vestibule of the church. For three years, He had a place in the back of the church with the unbaptized catechumens. When he was finally allowed to enter the church, he still had to pray prostrate until he was received back into fellowship.

We can be thankful such a practice has been eliminated but it is unfortunate that we do have church members who would like to see the sinner squirm awhile before full forgiveness is given. Jesus is the friend of sinners. If the church is to represent Jesus in the world, it must be known as the friend of sinners. If Judas would have gone to Jesus instead of to the church of his day, things could have been different for him. We will probably be surprised at the number of people in hell because full and complete pardon by word and deed was not given to those who were sorry for their sin. We will also be surprised at the number of people in heaven because they saw God's pardon in the way we forgave them. However, do not use the church as an excuse for not accepting God's pardon.

Some may find themselves in a trap of their own making. They had thought of themselves as forgiven and yet were unforgiving toward others. Other people commit sins, they think, that they would never become guilty of. They, so they think, are more worthy of forgiveness because their sins are not so great. This must be seen as spiritual pride and, in reality, faith in one's own works. The thought is: "I will never need that much forgiveness." However, such people are in deep trouble if they ever commit a sin which they believed to be the unpardonable sin of someone else. When a person like this does commit a sin of this nature, he must be led to believe that God is much more forgiving than he has been.

We can think of another case of spiritual pride. This person may believe he is forgiven and does have a forgiving attitude toward others. No sinner is too great a sinner and no person is too low. He loves them and readily forgives them. He knows people have problems and conditions can be such that they can be led to commit a sin for which they will later be sorry. He knows they are but human beings. Yet this same person can be unforgiving toward himself if he does commit a sin of any magnitude. The reason is that he may have felt he was always a little above all the rest. Some psychologists will tell you that when you cannot forgive yourself, you are a conceited person. You have placed yourself above the human race. You have said in your thoughts: "Others may do it, but not me." When a man with such pride sins, he needs to hear it said, "Welcome to the human race, son of Adam."

As we stand at the cross of Christ, sins are never too great or too many. "Where sin increased, grace abounded all the more" (Rom. 5:20). In almost any city, you could build a church and fill it with people who are overpowered with feelings of guilt. Many of these will have had a Christian upbringing. They may think of Jesus on the cross and have sorrow in their hearts for having caused Him all that pain by their sins. They cannot look Jesus in the eye. They feel unworthy to be in His presence and unworthy to be in His church. As a result, the forgiveness of God is not accepted by them.

If we think of the fact that Jesus suffered and died for all sins, would our sins ever be so great that we could not come to Him? Even if you have sorrow for having caused Him all that pain, does it do Him or you any good to go on living in unbelief? He has already suffered for all your sins anyway—past, present, and future. Does it not make more sense to accept the pardon of God now even though you may think your sins are greater than anyone else's? Then through the power of God's forgiveness you will be given freedom to live a better life in the future. Jesus died for sinners. He said on one occasion to the Pharisees: "The tax-gatherers and harlots will get into the kingdom of God before you" (Luke 21:31). They were sinners and they knew it, but they also knew Jesus as the Savior of sinners. If you think of yourself as a sinner or even a terrible sinner, you are the kind of person Jesus came to save. Jesus says, "Come to Me, all who are weary and heavy-laden, and I will give you rest" (Matt. 11:28). If your problem has been described above, take hold of the promise of Jesus, "The one who comes to Me I will certainly not cast out" (John 6:37).

God goes to great lengths to lead people to trust in Christ alone for salvation and to keep them in saving faith. God is serious about pledging us His forgiveness. Our baptism was for the "forgiveness of sins" (Acts 2:38). In the Lord's Supper, we receive Christ's body given and His blood shed for the "forgiveness of sins" (Matt. 26:26-28). Every Sunday on the basis of our confession, we hear of God's forgiving love for Jesus' sake. This is based on Jesus' words, "Receive the Holy Spirit. If you forgive the sins of any, their sins have been forgiven them . . ." (John 20:22-23). God seeks to convince us that the garment provided by Jesus on the cross covers each and every sin.

God's love and forgiveness is the power of the church. It is the duty of every pastor and every member of the church to lead others to a certain knowledge of their own forgiveness. Only the Holy Spirit can give and sustain saving faith. Yet we are still responsible for teaching, preaching, and persuading of men; even fellow members. We need to speak to the spiritual needs that men have so as to lead them to trust in Christ alone for their salvation and experience full and complete forgiveness before God.

The lack of assurance of forgiveness keeps the church from becoming "like a mighty army." If every church member would say, "I know I have sinned against God," and if every church member could say in his heart, "I know I am forgiven, I know I am going to heaven when I die, because I know that Jesus has lived, died, and rose again for my sins," the church would come alive with new life and power. Heaven for many people is an uncertain hope, wishful thinking, and perhaps much like a dream, and all of this because of the uncertainty of their own forgiveness. Assurance of forgiveness and eternal life always bring peace and joy. Where there is peace and joy, there is also life and power.

A young man, after hearing the presentation of the gospel, declined the invitation to receive Christ by saying, "I don't really understand what it means." When it came time for our next adult membership class, we debated as to whether or not to invite him to come. We decided to invite him, and as it turned out, he was one of the most faithful members of the class. After the class sessions were over, I visited his home again and asked him if he would now like to invite Christ into his life. He did not hesitate at all, and I led him in prayer. He did not join our church at the time since he moved away to another town. However, we were later given ample reason to believe he had received the assurance of salvation. I received five letters from him and each one contained a gift of $100 for the church. At Thanksgiving time, he said in his letter that he had so much for which to be thankful. In a Christmas letter, he said that Christmas had taken on a new meaning for him. In all five letters, there was always one statement which said, "Thank you for bringing me the Gospel." The money was always given to "support evangelism so that others may know the joy of Christ as their Savior."

"The joy of knowing Christ as their Savior!" Do you have this joy? It is serious when we do not have the assurance of our own forgiveness and eternal welfare. It is serious because it hurts us and diminishes the power which the church is to have. When we do not have assurance, we must stop trusting in ourselves so we are able to trust in Christ alone. We must stop worrying about the greatness of our sin and believe the precious blood of Christ to be of greater value than any debt we owe. "God so loved the world, that He gave His only begotten Son, that whoever believes in Him shall not perish but have eternal life" (John 3:16). God's love, His forgiveness through His Son, is the only way we could have "a garment as white as snow." God has promised us forgiveness and eternal life if we would believe in His Son. God says, "Because My Son has died and rose again, your sins are forgiven." Either this is accepted as true or we call God a liar. Remember, "God, who cannot lie, promised . . ." (Titus 1:2). Say with St. Paul, "Let God be found true, though every man be found a liar . . ." (Rom. 3:4).

When someone asks you why you hope to go to heaven, say, "I believe in—the forgiveness of sins." And if you are asked, "Can you give me a reason why God should forgive your sins?" point to the cross. It was there Jesus earned the right for you to be forgiven by suffering the punishment which you deserved. "All of us like sheep have gone astray, Each of us has turned to his own way; But the Lord has caused the iniquity of us all to fall on Him" (Is. 53:6).

There is forgiveness for you—believe it. God has provided "a garment as white as snow" for you through the blood of His Son—wear it. As you experience this gift of God day after day, more power will come into your life, and as it comes into your life, it will also flow into the life of the church.

> Jesus, Thy blood and righteousness
> My beauty are, my glorious dress;
> Midst flaming worlds, in these arrayed,
> With joy shall I lift up my head.

Bold shall I stand in that great Day,
For who aught to my charge shall lay?
Fully thro' these absolved I am
From sin and fear, from guilt and shame.

Lord, I believe were sinners more
Than sands upon the ocean shore,
Thou hast for all a ransom paid,
For all a full atonement made.

When from the dust of death I rise
To claim my mansion in the skies,
E'en then this shall be all my plea;
Jesus hath lived and died for me. TLH 371

1. The New Schaff-Herzog Encyclopedia of Religious Knowledge, Baker Book House, Grand Rapids, Mich., vol. Ill, 1940 page 236.

Chapter 5

Into the Word

I BELIEVE WE as Christians want to have God's power in our lives. We want a stronger faith, and we pray, "Lord, give me a strong faith." The desire and the prayer are good; but we have to keep in mind that God does not increase our faith without means. There is no example in the Bible where God converted a man with one stroke of His power and with the second gave him all power and knowledge. When we pray for a stronger faith, we need to look to the doors through which God sends His power into our hearts and lives. We call these doors the means of grace; they are the Word and Sacraments. In this book, we will be discussing only the power of the Word in our lives.

Where has all the power gone? Each chapter of this book is intended to show us a major reason for power loss. There are some ways in which we lose the power; but there are other ways in which the power is never received. In this chapter, we are talking about the power we do not receive because we are not involved in the Word as we should be. The big question is: "Why are we not receiving the power of God through the Word which He has given to us?" The obvious answer is: "Because we are not using it."

The Bible was never intended to be a good luck charm, a mantle piece, a place to press confirmation flowers, or a file to save newspaper clippings. From our earliest days, we have learned that the way we are to use our Bibles is to hear it, to learn it, and to meditate upon it. Another way of saying it was: "We should diligently and reverently read and study the Bible, listen attentively when it is read and explained, believe it, and live accordingly to it."1 There are at least seven ways to use the Word: Hear (listen), read, study, learn (memorize), meditate, believe it, and live it. For our purpose, let us think only of the input. We should know that believing the Word and living by the Word are absolutely essential to benefit from it; but we have people who believe it and who would live by it if they only knew what it was saying. Let us look then at the five ways in which the Word can come into our lives to have an effect upon us.

We hear the Word as we listen to the sermon on Sunday morning and as our teachers teach us. We study the Word not only by listening in Bible class but also when we do research on our own. We do study the Bible in a class even though we may not be prepared, but we receive much more value when we are prepared when we attend. People who teach Sunday school and Bible classes tell us how much they learn while they are preparing for their classes. Where did we ever get the idea that only the teacher has to be prepared? We read the Word simply by taking our Bibles in our own time and letting God speak to us day by day. We learn and memorize it by simply committing certain passages of Scripture to memory. This is valuable for it permits God to speak His Word to us when we do not have a Bible with us. We meditate on the Word when we think about what it is saying to us in our lives today. What did it mean then? What does it mean for us now?

If we would take these five ways of benefiting from the Word and put them into practice, most people would be surprised at the change that would come into their lives. Maybe we cannot say that each one is equally as important as the other, yet for illustration purposes, let us say that each way of benefiting from the Word equals 20 percent of your total growth potential. If you only hear the Word, then you are operating at 20 percent of your possible growth rate. A vast number of people use only this resource for their growth in faith. When you consider the tremendous drain on faith which comes to a person throughout the week through temptation and sin, it should lead us to wonder how faith could even exist, let alone grow. Without knowing any statistics, we might be safe in assuming that most congregations are realizing only about 30 percent of their potential growth rate. With perhaps less than 10 percent of our members in Bible Study every Sunday, with about 55 percent of our members in church, with a goodly number attending once a month or less, it is easy to see the need for improvement. What a tremendous event would take place if we could add a 70 percent increase in our receiving the Word of power for our faith and life!

Let us go back to the former illustration of the bucket of water; the water being faith, and the holes in the bucket being sins we have committed. Let us now add to this that using the Word is like pouring water into the bucket. This gives us an example of our faith as it waxes and wanes in our lives. A person who is careless about the kind of life he is living and uses the Word very little can hardly have a strong faith. Another person may be deeply involved in the Word, but is careless about his living. He is by no means realizing his full potential. The same would be true for the man who is careful about his living but careless about the Word. But when a person diligently and reverently uses the Word of God and is serious about his repentance and the receiving of forgiveness through Christ, his faith can flourish as a palm tree near springs of water.

There are several things which have kept the people of God from the Word. In recent years, liberal theologians have shocked the faith of some people by insinuating that the Bible should not be expected to be historically accurate. Some people stopped going to Bible Class when text books seemed to be denying the infallibility of Scripture. Their faith was shaken when they heard that perhaps Jonah was fictional, that the creation account was not necessarily literal, and that what was presented in some cases could not possibly have happened. How could lay people be expected to get excited about the prospect of having to sort out God's word from what might be human opinion? It is also a hindrance to the study of the Word when pastors are thought of as the infallible interpreters of the Word. If laymen believe they are dependent upon the pastor for an interpretation, they will be led to think: "Why bother to read the Bible on my own?" We can be thankful for modern day translations which have made the Word clearer to us all. Another hindrance was when theologians were insinuating that pastors were not well enough equipped to understand the deep theological questions of the day. If this were true of the pastor with five to seven years of training, what about the poor lay person? I know there are many things that we can learn which throw light on what the Bible is saying. I do not believe, however, that what we see in the Word will change much from what Grandma saw in it fifty years ago. While research into the shepherd-sheep relationship can add some spice to our thinking; yet not too much is added to the clear statement of Jesus when He said, "My sheep hear my voice, and I know them, and they follow Me; and I give eternal life to them, and they shall never perish; and no one shall snatch them out of My hand" (John 10:27-28). We should be in favor of scholarly work, but against the kind that would smother lay incentive.

Our liberal leaning in recent years, and the problems that have come as a result of it, should be seen as a judgment of God upon us for our failure to realize the potential of God's Word in our everyday lives. What is not used is lost. In our day, we see churches which have lost the Word. Some are in the process of losing it. In every instance, liberal theology is involved; but it is not necessarily the cause. Bible-believing Christians are not going to win the battle by finding the best arguments to use against them. We will win the battle only as we prove to God that His Word is the most precious thing in our lives. Recently, a pastor used this illustration for the children in a service. He had toys that children would play with and he asked two children to pick the toy they liked best. One picked a football and the other a doll. Then he asked, "How would you prove to me that you like the doll?" The answer was, "By playing with it." Then he asked the other, "How do you prove to me that you like the football?" And the answer again was, "By playing with it." In other words, by using the toy, they were proving they liked it. Then the pastor brought out the Bible, and asked the same question, "How do you prove to me that you like the Bible?" Here the answer was, "By reading it."

It is not proof of our love of the Bible by only saying, "I love the Bible. It is infallible. It is precious." God cannot be fooled by a superficial saying of words. God sees our love for His Word by our use of it. The Word that is not appreciated can be taken from us. It has happened to others. It can happen to us. Think of these Words of God, "'Behold, days are coming,' declares the Lord God, 'When I will send a famine on the land, not a famine for bread or a thirst for water, but rather for hearing the words of the Lord. People will stagger from sea to sea, and from the north even to the east; they will go to and fro to seek the word of the Lord, but they will not find it'" (Amos 8:11-12). We do not want to lose the Word. It is the only lamp to guide our feet in this sin-laden world. This is being discovered today. Men are setting aside the laws of God on many moral issues; but they end up puzzled wondering whose rules they are to follow. There are no rules once God's Word is set aside.

We are told: "Search the Scriptures . . ." (John 5:39). "Like newborn babes, long for the pure milk of the word . . ." (1 Peter 2:2). We have been told to read the Bible. We have been given examples of Bible reading. Paul and Silas came to Berea and we are told that "they received the word with great eagerness, examining the Scriptures daily, to see whether these things were so" (Acts 17:11). They were involved in reading and studying. In many churches today, the pastor could pull the wool over the eyes of the people because they are not loving the Word, respecting the Word, and using the Word.

We hear it said often, "I don't read the Bible because I don't understand it." There can be two reasons why this statement is made. First, they may not be born-again Christians, and because of this, they do not understand the main teaching of the Bible. The main teaching of the Bible is that "Salvation is a free gift of God as a result of Jesus taking our sins upon Himself and suffering and dying for them on the cross." If this is not known, Scriptures will be obscure. Secondly, a person may not be understanding the Bible because at the time, he is reading in Leviticus or Ezekiel. There are a few books of the Bible that are hard to understand. On the other hand, I do not know of anyone, except the illiterate, who could not read the gospel of John without profit. Even children can understand it. When a person says, "I can't understand it," he is agreeing with the ancient Roman Catholic Church. They chained the Bible in a library for fear that people might get the wrong understanding. For many Christians, the Bible might just as well be chained in the library for all the use they are getting out of it.

Another excuse for not reading the Bible might be, "Well, I have read it once." In this way, some people treat the Bible like the newspaper which is very valuable until you have read it; but after you have read it, it only becomes a burden as to what to do with it. In the first place, I do not know of anyone who has accumulated all Bible knowledge by reading it once. We forget many of the things we have read. Also, by reading it more than once, our memory is refreshed, and we will see things that were not seen in previous readings. The more we read the Bible, the easier it becomes to use it, and the more it becomes a part of our thinking and doing.

Those, however, who use the above excuse generally are thinking of only one aspect of the Bible. This is the knowledge they acquire by reading it. They overlook entirely the effect it has on their lives. It should be thought of as a powerful Word to create, sustain, and strengthen faith. Jesus said, "The words that I have spoken to you are spirit and are life" (John 6:63). The Word of God is a spiritual word, a life-giving word. This is much of the meaning of the words of Jesus when He said, "I am the vine, you are the branches; he who abides in Me, and I in him, he bears much fruit; for apart from Me you can do nothing" (John 15:5). As we read the Word, the Vine is nourishing us, the branches. If we disconnect ourselves from the Word, we are disconnecting ourselves from the Vine, and our faith will wither and die. All of us have this need for nourishment from the Vine, not just once a week, but every day of our lives.

We need the power of the Word to convince us of sin. Sometimes people will brush aside the attempts of others or even of pastors who try to show them some sin in their lives. They can give reasons why they do not agree with the evaluation; but the Word of God is more difficult to evade. "God's Word lives and is active. It cuts better than any two-edged sword. It pierces till it divides soul and spirit, joints and marrow. And it can judge thoughts and purposes of the heart. No creature can hide from Him. Everything is naked and helpless before the eyes of Him to whom we must give account" (Beck, Hebr. 4:12-13). Not only does it convince us of sin; but it also builds our faith. Saving faith is strengthened as we come across a passage like 1 John 1:7-9: "The blood of Jesus His Son cleanses us from all sin. If we say that we have no sin, we are deceiving ourselves and the truth is not in us. If we confess our sins, He is faithful and righteous to forgive us our sins and to cleanse us from all unrighteousness." It would be difficult to see how our faith for temporal things would not be strengthened by the Words of Jesus, "Your heavenly Father knows that you need all these things" (Matt. 6:32) or by the Words of Paul, "My God shall supply all your needs according to His riches in glory in Christ Jesus" (Phil. 4:19). Having read the Bible several times, I find that what was irrelevant at one time can become very relevant under different circumstances.

There is also a difference in using the Word for others and using it for yourself. Lay teachers can be led to think that since they are involved in the study of the Word for their classes, their use of the Word is sufficient. Pastors may think they are using the Word enough as they prepare their sermons or for Bible classes. However, this preparation is most often directed toward others. We need times when we permit the Word to speak to us directly. I will always be thankful to those people who led me to see the need of permitting God to speak to me and to my needs every day. God needs to show me personally my sin, my Savior, and the One I can trust when all else fails.

While there are many methods of reading the Bible, I would like to share with you the way that has been most beneficial to me. At the present time, I have three markers in my Bible, with two in the Old Testament and one in the New Testament. When I read the Old Testament, I do not start with Genesis and read it all the way through to Malachi. Rather, I put one marker in a book that is easy to read and one in a difficult book. We need to admit that some books at a given time are more beneficial to us than others. I try to read two chapters in each location each day with a minimum of one each. In this way, I do not lose interest in a particularly difficult section and stop reading. It is an aid to reading the whole Bible with profit. The difficult portions need to be read also because they are more valuable to us than we usually think. In this way, I find that God almost always has something valuable to say to me each day. In the New Testament, I have only one marker and I read only one chapter a day. I ration this since it is the most precious to me. I do not want to fly through it and not see it again for six months. And again, I do not read it from Matthew through Revelation. I will read Matthew and then Romans, Mark and then 1 Corinthians. In this way, I do not read the life of Christ four times in a row and not see it for a long period of time. Rather, I read a story about the life of Christ and then a letter of St. Paul, and then back again to another story of the life of Christ.

As we begin our reading, we should pray for the Lord's blessings upon us. Perhaps something like this: "Lord, I need Your Word in my life. Speak to me now and fill those needs that I will have in my life today." You may want to pray a hymn verse like the following:

Speak, O Lord, Thy servant heareth,
To Thy Word I now give heed;
Life and spirit Thy Word beareth,
All Thy Word is true indeed.

Death's dread pow'r in me is rife;
Jesus, may Thy Word of Life
Fill my soul with love's strong fervor
That I cling to Thee forever. TLH 296

Some might say, "Well, I don't have time." But the Campus Crusade Organization has shown that all we need is seven minutes to have a helpful devotion with God. It would seem absurd for someone to say that he cannot arise in the morning seven minutes earlier than usual. In seven minutes, you can have prayer and can read at least one chapter of the Bible. Many people, trying this method, have expanded the time they spend with God each morning.

I have seen young and old grow rapidly in knowledge and faith when they began reading the Bible regularly. I can give my own personal testimony of what it has meant for me to let God speak to me through His Word. He has strengthened my faith to trust Him in time of need. He has given me Words to say when someone else was experiencing a crisis in his life. He has assured me and continues to assure me of my salvation through faith in the Lord Jesus Christ. He has led me to see myself as I really am and has inspired me to do more and greater things for Him. I have never liked the song "I Come to the Garden Alone" because it seems to say that God works in us without means. The chorus, however, could be a beautiful description of how it is when we spend time each day reading God's Word and aware of His presence as we are doing it.

And He walks with me, and He talks with me, And He tells me I am His own, And the joy we share as we tarry there, None other has ever known.

There are times when a person cannot decide what to do. I have come to think of those times as times when God is trying to get our attention. He wants to speak to us through His Word. When your family cannot decide whether to go camping or visiting relatives, and you really do not know what to do, maybe it is God's way of ringing your number; wanting a conversation with you. I have mentioned this to my children when they say, "What can I do? There is just nothing to do." I say, "Maybe your Father in heaven wants to talk to you."

Some people feel useless in the world as far as the kingdom of God is concerned, and maybe they are. Maybe it is sin that clouds their witness or keeps them from witnessing. Maybe it is that they do not really have the assurance of their own salvation. Maybe it is because they are not at all prepared to be God's servants in the world. If the Word of God is not a part of our lives, if we are not reading it, believing it, and acting upon it, it would be difficult to see how God could use us to bring some message from His Word to someone in need of it. If we are not being used, then, at least, we ought to be preparing so we can be used at a later date. God will use us, if we will only be faithful in the use of His Word: hearing, reading, studying, meditating, and memorizing it.

There is an energy crisis in the material world today; but there is also an energy crisis in the spiritual world. It is not that energy is not available. It is that the source of energy is not being tapped. If every member would get serious about the Word of God, the church's power could be increased fourfold. Four times as much power is certainly something to work for and something to pray for. Our faith can be weak and our faith can even die for lack of spiritual food. "Faith comes from hearing, and hearing by the word of Christ" (Rom. 10:17). So it is, "Into the Word" or die; or put more positively, "Into the Word" and come alive. If you are convinced, then convince someone else of the need of a daily and of a fuller use of the living, active, and powerful Word of God.

> Lord, Thy words are waters living
> Where I quench my thirsty need;
> Lord, Thy words are bread life-giving,
> On Thy words my soul doth feed.
> Lord, Thy words shall be my light

Thro' death's vale and dreary night;
Yea, they are my sword prevailing
And my cup of joy unfailing.

Precious Jesus, I beseech Thee,
May Thy words take root in me;
May this gift from heav'n enrich me
So that I bear fruit for Thee!
Take them never from my heart
Till I see Thee as Thou art,
When in heav'nly bliss and glory
I shall greet Thee and adore Thee. TLH 296

1. Luther's Small Catechism, 1965 Edition, Concordia
   Publishing-House, St. Louis, Missouri, Page 42.

Chapter 6

Into The Closet

ONE GREAT SIN of omission is when we do not pray. Samuel, an Old Testament prophet, wrote, "Far be it from me that I should sin against the Lord by ceasing to pray for you . . ." (1 Sam.12:23). If we say, "There is great power in prayer," most people will agree; but unfortunately we experience very little of the power available to us. When we ask, "Where has all the power gone?" it is again not a matter of losing power. Rather, it is a failure on our part to appropriate the power that is available to us. We do not use the avenue which God has opened to us by the sacrificial death of His Son. Jesus said, "If you ask the Father for anything in My name, He will give it to you" (John 16:23), "And all things you ask in prayer, believing, you shall receive" (Matt. 21:22). Is your church a praying church? This question could be confusing to many church members. Some might answer yes thinking about the prayer led by the pastor every Sunday morning. Some might say no thinking of individual members whom they have never witnessed leading in prayer. Some would, no doubt, say, "I don't know." This is the position I would take as I think of my church as a whole. Many individual church members may very well be praying fervently every day. It is a problem, however, when we do not know if people are practicing the art of prayer.

I see it as a problem because people have said to me, "I will pray for you," and I have walked away wondering if it was just a figure of speech wishing me well. When some have said they would pray for me, I cherished the promise because I had come to know them as people who prayed. I knew they would do what they said. I was told once of a possible solution to this problem. If someone says he will pray for you, our answer should be, "Great! How about right now?" I would hesitate to do this because a goodly number of those who say this could not lead you in prayer on the spot. My wife put a twist on this. A friend, who was expressing a great deal of concern over a personal problem said, "Will you remember me in your prayers?" My wife was quick to respond, "How about right now?" The door was closed, and a prayer was said in an office of a public building. What a changed world we would have if every child of God would practice this priestly function (1 Peter 2:9).

A song which has troubled me as it is sung in church is "Sweet Hour of Prayer." It troubles me because I feel that most of us have never experienced one hour in prayer. Many have not even experienced one difficult hour of prayer and yet we sing "sweet" hour of prayer as if this has had some special meaning for us. Many church members hold the thought that if we sing about something it is as if we are doing it. We get into the area of knowing of and agreeing with a practice, but never in reality practicing it. A person can grow up singing hymns in this way. When children sing hymns, as cute as they may sound, they are most often singing about experiences they have never had. We can grow up into adulthood doing the same thing. We are able to sing about a sweet hour of prayer without ever having had one.

Jesus is our perfect example. He prayed early in the morning (Mark 1:35). Before calling the twelve men to be His Apostles, He prayed all night (Luke 6:12-13). I cannot even visualize myself praying all night. While I have worked to improve my prayer life, I know there is still much more to learn. I was involved once in a prayer sixty miles long. I have a habit of praying aloud as I drive alone in the car. On this particular morning, I had something on my mind bothering me. It was sixty miles to my destination so I prayed all the way.

We need to study the examples given of the prayer life of Jesus. We sing in the Lenten hymn, "Learn of Jesus Christ to pray." The Apostles noticed His prayer life. They, no doubt, took note of how He would go to prayer, troubled in mind and spirit, and would return again refreshed. They could see the value of prayer for Him, and this led to their request, "Lord, teach us to pray . . ." (Luke 11:1). A desire to pray is the first step toward a prayer life. We need to ask the Lord to teach us to pray, and then work at it. When you hear an idea that sounds good and proper, put it into practice.

The Bible gives many examples of men in prayer. Before I began writing this chapter, I was given an excellent example of a man who prayed. Most of the time, I begin a particular work with prayer, asking the Lord's blessing upon what I will be doing. So before I began writing this morning, I prayed. This was followed by reading one chapter from the Bible. I turned to my second marker in the Old Testament, and it was the first chapter of Nehemiah. It is an example of prayer. While Nehemiah was in captivity, he received a report of how things were in Jerusalem. The people were in "great distress," the walls of Jerusalem were "broken down" and the gates were "burned with fire." What did Nehemiah do? "When I heard these words, I sat down and wept and mourned for days; and I was fasting and praying before the God of heaven" (Neh. 1:1-4). If only we could receive bad news this way, be led to weep and mourn, and then to plead with the God of heaven. A similar example is found in 1 Samuel 15:10: "Samuel was distressed and cried out to the Lord all night."

Our church body has gone through, or perhaps we can say, is still going through a severe trial. What a change could take place if, instead of griping about this person and complaining about that situation, we would weep and mourn and pray to our Father in heaven. We would witness a remarkable change in our own lives, but also in the life of our church. We would witness a remarkable happening in each of our congregations if this art could be practiced. Nothing takes away from enthusiasm more than a person who is constantly complaining and fault-finding. One Sunday morning, I was enthused about the possibilities of our Sunday school and worship service. In my heart, I was singing "Happy am I" on the way to church; but you know, it took one person about two minutes to wipe out my enthusiasm. Sure, we need to hear legitimate complaints; but complaints without a possible solution are death to joy in the church. Complaints which have not passed through the heart of God by a considerable time in prayer are death to enthusiasm. No complaint should be made without prayer. Through prayer, God would discard from our hearts many of the complaints we have.

Jesus said, "My house shall be called a house of prayer . . ." (Matt. 21:13). Is your church a house of prayer? The average church of today is considered having a holy atmosphere one hour each week on Sunday morning; but I have a dream for my church. Someday, I would like to walk into one of our churches and catch someone in the act of praying. Right now I feel like I would walk up to the person and say, "Can I join you in prayer?" Have you ever gone by yourself to your church to pray? Have you ever had the strange feeling that someone is going to walk in and find out what you are doing? I have had this uneasy feeling myself; but I think it comes from years of experience of never seeing the church used for praying. In this area, I truly admire a church of the Roman Catholic persuasion. When you walk into one of their churches, you are automatically quiet because you expect to find someone praying there.

I wish our churches were this way. We may be in danger of not adopting a practice simply because another denomination has it. We do not have to adopt someone else's prayers or way of praying; but we can and should adopt the practice of praying in church. Be assured, rather than being harmed, that great benefits will come. We need to use every method available to teach each member of our churches the art of daily communication with God. It is my prayer that someday our church in convention will pass a resolution to "encourage all churches to include in their building plans a prayer chapel or to provide a suitable place in the Sanctuary which can be used by individual members for prayer." I am sure most congregations would find twenty-five or fifty people who would use these places; using it more often than we can now realize. It would not be long and every member would be aware of the changed atmosphere in the church every day of the week. The ones who were already involved with personal prayer could give boldness to others. If churches have to be locked, there could be set times when they would be open for prayer.

Power is available to us as individual Christians and for the church. It is not being experienced because we are not utilizing it. The real potential of our praying is not through the prayer offered on Sunday morning as we are gathered together. It is important, but the real potential is when every member is praying throughout the week. To develop the art of praying, we need to have prayer lists. Because I cannot remember all the things which I feel need prayer, I use such a list. I had mentioned before that I use three markers in the Bible. These are really prayer lists. Some of my prayers are typed. One, for example, is for the church: "Lord, prosper Thy Church. Let Thy Word be preached with power. Convert those who are not yet Thine. Make those who are Thine, wholly Thine, filling them with love, zeal, and the spirit of sacrifice for Thy kingdom." I do not remember where I saw this prayer, but at the time, I felt it was good; covering a lot of territory in a few words. I typed it on a card and placed it in my Bible. Under this prayer, I have written the names of three men. My son and his friend in preseminary training at Ann Arbor, Michigan, and a nephew at the seminary in Fort Wayne, Indiana.

On one card, I have prayer prompters. At one time, you had to prime a pump by pouring water into it before you could pump any water out. The prayer prompters do this for me as I seek to pray to God. One example is the little statement, "Lord, forgive—." This gives me the opportunity to pray for someone who has caused me some discomfort. I ask God to forgive the one who wronged me and to help me also to forgive. The petitions of the Lord's Prayer could be used as prompters to use the best prayer to move us to many prayers. Besides these things, I jot down various things on these cards which I feel need prayers.

Our family is now in the process of developing another aid to

individual prayer in our home. We have a family prayer list. We are far from reaching its potential; but we are working on it. A book could be written on this one item alone. We placed a prayer list in a prominent location. Prayer suggestions were written on it as we felt the need. The rule was that when you had prayed for one item you would put your initials and date by it. Another rule was that before it was considered to be a prayer, you had to read one chapter of the Bible before or after your prayer. On our first list, we had eighteen things for which to pray. When we felt we had the answer, we would write PTL, meaning Praise the Lord, on it. Of those eighteen petitions, we had eight PTLs. For some of these, we would probably never see an observable answer, as for example, we put our married daughter's family on the list. We assume the Lord is blessing their household as a result of our prayers. This prayer list has helped our family to believe that God answers prayers and sometimes in amazing ways. We admit that we have not observed answers for all of our prayers. We had prayed one petition eighteen times without an observable answer. We had an answer to another prayer after twenty-one times.

Maybe some church has this now; but I could see a real blessing for any church that has a prayer chapel to develop such a prayer list. Suggestions could be made for the prayer list by any member of the congregation with all requests being channeled through the pastor and elders.

Jesus said, "But thou, when thou prayest, enter into thy closet, and when thou hast shut thy door, pray to thy Father which is in secret; and thy Father which seeth in secret shall reward thee openly" (King James Version, Matt. 6:6). When Jesus was talking about a closet, He was not talking about our present day closets. If we would go into our closets today and close the door, we would suffocate. Modern translations will read "inner room" or "inner chamber" with the idea being a private place. When Jesus says, "Go into your closet," it means "Be alone when you are talking to your Father in prayer." The reason Jesus spoke these words was to keep us from grandstanding in our prayer life. But I think that it was more than this. Jesus knew how valuable it would be for anyone of His followers to have a private prayer life. When you are alone with God, you can talk to God more openly and honestly than you can in any other circumstance. We can be and should be open and honest in our praying with others; but there will always be some things that you want to talk about only when you are alone with your heavenly Father. This is the best place to develop your prayer life—to learn how to pray. We need to develop our prayers even if we are alone with God. We need to say our prayers in words and not just in thoughts.

Some people cannot pray for an extended period of time because they think of prayer as only being the petition, that is, what we want and for which we are asking. A prayer of this nature goes something like this: "Lord, give me a new car." People walk away from such a prayer thinking that this is all there is to prayer. When we pray, there should be several things involved. If you cannot remember them, write them on a card. There should be a confession of all known sins so that no sin stands between us and our God. There should be the assuring of ourselves that through the forgiveness of Jesus Christ, there is nothing that will hinder our prayer. There should be thanksgiving to God for His past blessings upon us, being specific about particular blessings. Then bring your request to God, followed by your praise for His goodness and greatness, and for the answer He will give.

Even in our petitions, we should add more than the request itself. If we look at the prayers of God's people given to us as examples in the Bible, we will see that they included in their prayers reasons why God should answer the prayer. This not only increases the length of time we spend with God, but it leads us to wrestle with God in prayer. As we are thinking of these reasons, we are involved in the consideration as to whether or not this could possibly be the will of God. For example, you may not be able to think of as many reasons for having a new car as you could for having an evangelism program started in your church.

When Moses prayed for the people of Israel at a time when God threatened to destroy them, he gave three reasons for God not to destroy them. In our thinking, we sort of chuckle saying that God already knows the reasons. God does know; but He wants us to see clearly the reasons why He would or should answer our prayer. These reasons we give, if they are good enough, can give us a stronger faith. We can talk ourselves into trusting God more for the answer. Think now of the three reasons given by Moses. He said, "Don't look at the stubbornness or the wickedness of this people. Remember Your servants, Abraham, Isaac, and Jacob." God had made them a promise concerning this people and the new land. When you take hold of God by His promise, you are in an excellent position. Another reason Moses gave for his prayer request was based on God's own honor. He was saying, "What will Egypt think? They will think that You were not able to do what You started out to do" (Deut. 9:28). Then the final reason for an answer to his prayer is what I call the master touch. He said, "They are Your people . . ." (Deut. 9:29). There are many things your child can be and do which embarrasses you; but one thing never changes; the child is still your child. No parent who loves his children will want something evil to happen to them. God is this way. His children are precious to Him. If we could learn to pray to God like Moses when we are in our closet, we would become extremely rich in our spiritual lives. Also, blessing upon blessing would be showered upon us and the world around us.

Nehemiah used similar reasons for his prayer request. He was living in the time of the captivity. The captivity was a result of the people's wickedness, and now Nehemiah was going to pray them out of captivity. He gave two reasons for God to answer His prayer. He said, "Remember the word which You commanded Your servant Moses . . . if you return to Me and keep My commandments and do them, though those of you who have been scattered were in the most remote part of the heavens, I will gather them from there and will bring them to the place where I have chosen to cause My name to dwell" (Neh. 1:8-9). The reason Nehemiah gave was based upon a promise of God. The other reason was the same as that given by Moses: "They are Your servants and Your people whom You redeemed by Your great power and by Your strong hand" (Neh.1:10). These reasons were given by Nehemiah telling God why He should soften the heart of the king from whom he was to get permission to rebuild the walls of Jerusalem.

You can read twenty-five books on prayer and not improve your prayer life unless you are willing to take a step and practice the things you have read and believed. When Jesus said, "Into the closet,"

He meant for every one of His followers to have a private prayer life with His Father and their Father. Since He has commanded us to pray, we are more than negligent if we do not. We are sinning, and someday we will realize just how great the sin has been. We, by not praying, become guilty for the lack of power in us and others. We have been told that we could not only dry up a fig tree but also move mountains if we had faith as small as a mustard seed. We are moving pebbles instead of mountains. God will unleash His power upon us and through us to others if we will only learn how to daily enter the closet and pray in secret to our Father in heaven. "Into your closet" and witness the power of God in our day as we have witnessed it in the new-born, spirit-filled, and infant church of our ascended and ruling Lord, Jesus Christ.

> Prayer is the Christian's vital breath,
> The Christian's native air,
> His watchword at the gates of death—
> He enters heaven with prayer.
>
> O Thou by whom we come to God,
> The Life, the Truth, the Way,
> The path of prayer Thyself hast trod—
> Lord, teach us how to pray. TLH 454

Chapter 7

With One or Two in His Name

I WILL ALWAYS remember the first prayer group with which I was involved. A man and his wife had a little girl with leukemia. They, my wife and I, and a friend of both families, decided to gather at the church for prayer in behalf of the child. We read a portion of the Bible, and then each one prayed a petition or petitions aloud. By the time we had finished praying, we had tear-filled eyes and runny noses. I could see two reasons for the tears. One was because of the love we had for this child. The other reason, I believe, was that our praying together was a fulfillment of the desires we had in our hearts. We had heard of others who had been involved in prayer groups, we had wanted this for ourselves, and now it had become a reality.

We continued to come together at different times and openly invited other members of the church to participate. While we did have visitors to our group, the five of us were the ones who kept the meetings going. Besides praying for the child, we began to pray for other things, for ourselves and for the church. The sad part of the story is that the child for whom we had gathered to pray did not recover. One night, Sherry died in her father's arms on the way to the hospital. However, this family had assurance of their girl's salvation. They knew Jesus had died for the sins of little children, no less than others. They knew she had been received into the kingdom of God through baptism. She had

grown up knowing Jesus, the Savior of all. I will never forget the scene
at the funeral home: the father, the head of the house, leading his wife
and other children in prayer beside the casket of their departed loved
one. This scene remains beautiful in my mind.

It was not that our prayer group failed. I believe that, as a result of
the prayer meetings, the church experienced a spiritual revival. I became
more involved in evangelism than I had ever been before. An evangelism
training program for the laymen was begun. At about the same time,
the Ongoing Ambassadors for Christ came to our congregation to
start their program in our circuit. I will never forget the day when
some of the youth of our circuit were being trained to witness door
to door with the temperature at twenty degrees below zero. Within
six months, six laymen had been involved in an evangelism training
program, and approximately twenty youth had learned how to witness
for their Savior. The youth began on their own a weekly Bible study
and prayer meeting. I have seen much suffering among God's people
which seemed to have no explanation. In the case of Sherry, I could see
a reason for her illness. It led some of us to gather together in the name
of Jesus to ask the Father to pour out a blessing upon us.

This was my initial interest in a group meeting for prayer. This
interest was increased as I became involved with the OAFC.(1) I saw
the leadership of this movement bow together for prayer asking the
Lord's blessings upon their youth training program. I saw the youth of
this organization growing rapidly in their spiritual lives as they openly
studied the Bible together. They poured out their hearts to the Lord for
themselves, for others, and for the movement to which they belonged.
They believe in prayer power. One summer, I led a group of these
youth as they went to Gering, Nebraska to start the program there.
We had two cars, and the youth riding with me often had a Bible
study and prayed together. We prayed always for a safe trip. We prayed
for the Holy Spirit's blessing upon us. We prayed for the churches
we would visit along the way, and we prayed for the big event—the
starting of the OAFC movement in Gering, Nebraska. We learned to

say "Praise the Lord" as we knew specific answers to requests we had made. These things have convinced me of the need for prayer meetings in our churches today.

Perhaps we do not have prayer meetings because this is something promoted in other denominations or by other movements. Fear, however, can keep us from doing the very thing our Lord wants, yes, even commanded us to do. There are many Christians today who yearn for an experience of an active spiritual life. If the spiritual desires of our people are not being met—praising the Lord, singing spiritual songs, praying with one another—only then will other groups and movements appear to be a threat to us.

Jesus said, "Where two or three have gathered together in My name, I am there in their midst" (Matt. 18:20). While this is not specifically referring to a prayer meeting, it most certainly means this also. We gather to work, to sing, to study, and to pray in Jesus' name. This passage indicates to us that it does not take fifty people to have a prayer meeting. You only need two. The OAFC movement began when two pastors, concerned about the youth of our day prayed together. The fact is that fifty in a group would be less effective than five or ten. If fifty people would gather for prayer, the meeting will be more effective if they were divided into groups of ten. The Bible does not really tell us how many were involved in prayer meetings. Some have the appearance of being large while others seem small.

For example, after Jesus had lived and died for our sins, rose again with power, and ascended into heaven in glory, we see the first example of a prayer meeting. In Acts 1:14, speaking about 120 people, it is said, "These all with one mind were continually devoting themselves to prayer, along with the women, and Mary the mother of Jesus, and with His brothers." It was upon this assembled, praying group that the Spirit was poured. A little later in Acts 4, we see another prayer meeting which resulted from persecutions. Some of the things about this event are significant. First, "When they heard this, they lifted their voices to God *with one accord . . ."* (italics mine). One of the keys to effective praying is being of one mind about what we are praying. Jesus said, "If two of you agree on earth about anything that they may ask, it shall be done for them by My Father who is in heaven" (Matt. 18:19).

We will not find oneness with other people as we will find with members of our own church. The Holy Spirit has called me to be a Christian and has placed me in a particular body of Christians called Lutherans. I am in agreement with all who hold to the historic Lutheran confessions. Being with Lutherans, it will not be necessary for me to discuss and debate our position on Baptism and the Lord's Supper. I also have a greater desire for my church to grow than others. This is not selfishness. While the Lord looks upon my family as being no more important than others, He does expect me to have the greatest concern for those He has given me. The Lord has given me my wife and children for me to love more than anyone else could love them in the world. The Lord wants me to love and teach them, but also to pray with and for them. So God has placed me in a larger family which we call a local Lutheran congregation and He expects me to love this family, to teach, to share, and to pray with and for them. So when we pray, being in agreement on doctrine, the only other thing we need is to agree on what we want the Lord to do in our midst.

What should we pray for? We can pray for anything except things that we know are from the devil. However, we should learn to change more to praying for spiritual things than we do. When the early church was persecuted, it did not pray for the persecution to stop. They prayed for courage to face it. It was a remarkable prayer receiving a remarkable answer. "When they had prayed, the place where they had gathered together was shaken, and they were all filled with the Holy Spirit and began to speak the word of God with *boldness*" (Acts 4:31, italics mine). We are often too materialistic minded when we pray, and as long as we think this way, we will seldom reach this "one accord" type praying. When we think like God thinks, when we want what God wants, and when we are doing what God wants done, we will begin to experience God's power as He answers our united prayers.

Who should be involved in a prayer group? Where should the prayer meetings be held? Every Christian should be involved in such meetings and these meetings can be held anywhere—in church, in a home, in the park, and even traveling down the road. I say every Christian should be involved because it is a learning experience. Just as laymen need on the job training in evangelism, so they also need on the job training in praying. If the whole church gathered for prayer, some of the Christians could pray aloud and others could not. The silent prayers need to be involved so they can learn from those who pray aloud. While prayers will always need to be improved, yet the most feeble attempt at praying should be acceptable in our midst. No one should feel condemned because of a faltering, stammering, prayer request. A lady came to our prayer meeting for the first time and between some of the other prayers, she tearfully threw out the words, "Lord, help my friend." While a prayer specialist could find a dozen things wrong with the prayer, the Lord would find the one thing right about it. It was a heart-felt prayer. She must, however, have embarrassed herself because she never came to another prayer meeting. Things like this should not happen. An artist, very seldom, is proud of his first attempt at painting. Preachers, very seldom, look back at their first sermons as prize-winning. When you are learning something in any field, your first attempts are usually poor; but if a person's heart is in it, he continues so as to improve. He is not embarrassed to the point of giving up.

We need to learn how to pray. Even if you know how to pray, you are still in the school learning better ways. You should plan to be there until the day you die. Just because someone else can sing better than I, does not keep me from singing. Just because others pray better than I do, and I have seen many who do, does not keep me from praying. Our pastors teach members that they are to pray, the form of prayer, and how to pray; but more is needed. The art of prayer needs to be practiced and nothing is better than actually attending a prayer meeting. If we could learn how to gather for prayer with one or two others in Jesus' name, we could experience the same kind of dynamic life as in the first church. Our faith would become stronger, our witness bolder, and our works more miraculous. James' statement "You do not have because you do not ask" (James 4:2) should ring in our ears. So many people are weeping. So many unnecessary burdens are borne. So many things go unprayed for.

The Bible gives us some touching scenes about prayer meetings.

On one occasion, the Elders of the church in Ephesus came to meet with Paul at Miletus. Paul was passing by, but he wanted a word with these leaders. He, first of all, spoke words of warning and encouragement to them. Then we are told of the final prayer meeting for Paul with this group: "When he had said these things, he knelt down and prayed with them all" (Acts 20:36). There was hugging, kissing, and crying; but there was more—there was praying. They were lovers of the Lord and lovers of one another, and so there was prayer.

There was another prayer meeting at Tyre. Paul was still on his way to Jerusalem, but he took the time to look up the disciples in the city. They ended the meeting with a Christian beach party. "After kneeling down on the beach and praying, we said farewell to one another" (Acts 21:5). These were "ex corde" (from the heart) prayers. We have counted on our written and our read prayers to bring to the Lord the concerns of our hearts. They do not always do that. Written prayers do not always say what I want to say. They are most often general rather than specific. They are prayers involving everyone and yet not completely satisfying anyone. On a world day of prayer, we resort to responsive readings so that everyone will be praying aloud; but sometimes even in these, we cannot always agree with what the writer has in mind. There is a need for our responsive prayers and for our general prayers that were read in church; but a greater need of the human heart is to pour out our requests to God with others. Their hearts can reach out to us and join us in our requests. We can feel closeness to one another as we together draw close to the Lord in prayer.

A person should go to a prayer meeting, if not to pray, to learn how to pray. It is an opportunity for people to talk about prayer and the things which will make our prayers more effective. It gives to us the opportunity to practice the art of prayer. It could lead to the time when every member of our churches would be able to lead others in prayer. Together, Christians need to discuss prayer goals. Goals should never be set so high that no one could believe it possible to reach. Goals should be reasonable. A person would find it difficult to believe as he would pray: "Lord, let me convert everyone in the world." On the other hand, a person could believe as he would pray: "Lord, give me one soul to love and to bring to You."

Together as Christians, we can seek God's guidance. For example, I wrote in one song, called "Dependence":

> Show to us, O Lord, the road to go
> Day by day, Your will for us to know
> To walk each day with power from above
> To live each day encircled by Your love
> To live each day encircled by Your love.

One congregation agreed with the pastor to have a month in which no meetings would be held except prayer meetings. The meetings were to be used to ask the Lord for directions as to what He wanted the congregation to do. They continued to have their worship services, but the only other meetings were the prayer meetings. We do ask for the Lord's blessings and guidance, but in my opinion, not nearly often enough. Proceedings of meetings should be interrupted when an empasse has been reached and prayer should be offered to God who will clear the way before us. Minute by minute, we need to live in the presence of our Heavenly Father whose ears are attentive to our every need. Jesus made it a possibility for us; and we need to pray that the Holy Spirit will make it a reality for us.

For quite sometime, our family has had its own prayer meetings. We have, on occasions, said, "We have a problem. Let us sit down and pray about it." Most often, our prayer meetings are held after supper, after we lave heard some word from God through a devotion or Scripture reading. Sometimes the devotion has a prayer. When it does, one member of the family will read it while the others in turn will offer a prayer of their own or a word of thanksgiving. We have had our share of difficulty in keeping this going. The devil, no doubt, would like to see it stopped. We have even become involved in arguments while we were getting ready to pray, but we have not let this stop us. I can see our family growing closer to the Lord.

We try not to make these devotions an absolute must. If we make it a legalistic type ritual, the children can grow up feeling they have to, and maybe not want to. One night after supper, I said that we did not have to have devotions since we were in a hurry. I feel this way. If a family is having devotions as a general rule, it is no catastrophe if they do not have it on a particular night. Anyway, after I had said this, my oldest daughter at home responded with "Dad!" Well, we had our devotions, but not because Dad said so, but because a daughter said so. We should see more of this. When our children begin to encourage us, then we need to say, "Praise the Lord."

My wife and I have prayed with one other person as a prayer group. We have prayed with another couple. The last time we moved to a new town, we prayed for God to give us some people with whom we could study the Bible and pray. The Lord answered those prayers. In fact, we are having a meeting tonight with two other couples. While our children, in this case, are playing together, we will be reading the Word and praying together. This means He has given to us friends in a new area; but more important, friends we know in Christ. This is not a substitute for other church activity. We will be in church on Wednesday night for a Lenten service, and then on Thursday night we plan to go to a church sponsored Bible study.

To enjoy religion and to spend much time doing religious things is what some would call fanatic. But religion can be exciting and fun. In fact, a person can have more fun doing spiritual things than many of the other things that we do in the world. It is also more satisfying.

Religion is fun if consistently practiced after the pattern given to us by the Lord Jesus. We can laugh together, weep together, and sing together as we gather in Jesus' name. It happens too often that youth endure the Bible study and afterwards have their fun, or ladies have their Bible study and then get down to the real purpose for coming together. This should be changed. Let the real purpose of our meetings be prayer and Bible study. Let us do it at times seriously, but more often with light hearts; just having a good time.

Praying in a group can be difficult for some. Part of the difficulty may be that some Christians do not have a good prayer life alone. If you never pray alone, it would be extremely difficult to pray with others. Being self-conscious can keep some from praying aloud. Being in a group, however, can lead a person to forget himself and to think about the needs of others, and especially the needs of the church.

Praying in a group, however, is beneficial. It leads us to pray for others rather than just praying for our own selfish needs.

It leads us to pray for what we most have in common: the kingdom of God and the salvation of souls. It leads us to pray more for spiritual things rather than the material. We discover what we have in common is more spiritual than material. And besides these things, we will be led to pray more often, to pray more unitedly and fervently, as we gather together with one or two in Jesus' name. The result would be the outpouring of God's blessings upon our Church and upon us as individuals. When alone, but also together in groups, let us:

Lift it up to Jesus, hold it before his eyes. You will see His goodness, come flowing from the skies.

Maybe the need for a prayer meeting will disappear if we could include in our other meetings a period of ten or fifteen minutes when individual Christians can pray for a need in the church as they see it. But as long as we feel this is too much time to spend in prayer in our meetings, there will be a need for a prayer meeting. And as long as there is a "need" for a prayer meeting, the church will endure a lack of power, and will endure it until one is started. The Lord can give us things without our praying for it; but He withholds many things to give them to us as a result of our praying. Then we will not have any doubt as to where our blessings come from. Prayers keep us from thinking that we accomplish things by our own intelligence and skill, and leads us to praise God from whom our every blessing flows. Where has all the power gone? This power promised by the Lord will come upon us again as the command of our Lord to pray is carried out as individuals and with one or two in His name.

> Our Father, Thou in heav'n above,
> Who biddest us to dwell in love,
> As brethren of one family,
> To cry in ev'ry need to Thee,
> Teach us no thoughtless words to say,
> But from our inmost heart to pray.

1. OAFC, Ongoing Ambassadors for Christ, Inc., 3009 Thomas, Wichita Falls, Texas 76308

Chapter 8

Out on a Limb

JESUS SAID, "GO into all the world and preach the gospel to all creation" (Mark 16:15). Most church members will agree that the main mission of the church is to preach the gospel. Do you know what the gospel is? It would be well for you to answer this question before reading on. I have had the opportunity to ask the young and old alike this question, and often without getting a good answer, and in some cases, getting no answer. If we do not know what the gospel is, how can we proclaim it to every creature? Some say the gospel is any good news coming into a bad situation. In other words, if you were to give $5.00 to a poor man to buy food for his family, it would be good news to him and the gospel according to some. However, while this is a good deed, and something to be practiced as a child of God, it is not the gospel. There are those who preach about Jesus, extending an invitation to accept Jesus, and do this with little or no gospel. The emphasis in many cases is on how Jesus will change your life, or on how different you will feel. People have told me about their going forward at a revival without understanding why they were doing it. They went forward and accepted Christ, but they still did not know Him as their Savior.

The very heart of the Gospel is found in the cry of Jesus on the cross, "My God, My God, why hast Thou forsaken Me?" You will not know the gospel until you know why the Father forsook His Son in that moment of history. You do not know the gospel unless you can tell people why Jesus suffered and died. Many people know that Jesus lived and died upon a cross, but very few people today know why. They know facts about the cross without knowing the substitutionary nature of it. The gospel is that God placed all our sins upon Jesus and punished Him in our stead. Isaiah's gospel was: Jesus was "stricken, smitten of God and afflicted . . . He was pierced through for our transgressions, He was crushed for our iniquities . . ." (Is. 53:4-5). The gospel according to Paul was: "Christ died for our sins . . . and that He was buried, and that He was raised on the third day . . ." (1 Cor. 15:3-4). Speaking of Jesus as our substitute, Paul wrote, "He made Him who knew no sin to be sin on our behalf, so that we might become the righteousness of God in Him" (2 Cor. 5:21). Peter's gospel was: "He Himself bore our sins in His body on the cross . . ." (1 Peter 2:24). The gospel, whether it is accepted or not, is that God's justice is satisfied completely because the penalty for sin has been fully paid. So now, when we proclaim the gospel, we must state a fact about the cross, "Jesus has died for your sins and for the sins of all men upon the cross." This gives people a reason for believing in Him.

If people accept Christ without understanding the gospel, they will be greatly disillusioned as they see little or no change in their lives. The Holy Spirit works genuine faith in the hearts of people as they see Jesus suffering and dying in their behalf. The Apostle Paul spoke of this gospel in his first chapter to the Corinthians. "For the word of the cross is foolishness to those who are perishing, but to us who are being saved it is the power of God" (1 Cor. 1:18). Today, there are many "sign" seekers who follow on the heels of the miracle workers whose main message is healing. An elderly lady went into great detail telling me about the four different times she was healed of four different bodily ailments. She did give all credit to Jesus for this. But when I asked her, "Why do you expect to go to heaven?" she did not have an answer. There are also those who are distributors of their great wisdom, showing with great skill how wrong the church is or has been, and often claiming a copyright on the interpretation of dark passages of Scripture. Most often this wisdom is peddled without any gospel witness. He, with Paul, must "preach Christ crucified" (1 Cor. 1:23). This simple proclamation is the "power of God."

The gospel is our weapon of warfare. It is a powerful weapon. Doubting this power is what leads some to change the form of the gospel, making it a social gospel, and others to do nothing at all. Many Christians give the impression that they are ashamed of the gospel. To think that all we have to do is to tell others that Jesus loves them and has died for them is foolishness to them. They think of it as a flimsy means of warfare, something like attacking the enemy with a paper sword. We do so little witnessing today because we have grave doubts as to the effectiveness of the gospel witness. We need to see it as the most powerful weapon God has ever placed into the hands of men. The gospel saves. Through the power of the Holy Spirit, the gospel creates saving faith as it is spoken. The power of God in the gospel changes lives. It rescues people from bondage and establishes them as the sons of God.

This chapter is called "Out on a Limb" because a person has to witness to experience God's power in and with the Gospel. Many of us have grown up in the church and have become accustomed to hearing the gospel. We have had no revolutionary experience as far as the good news is concerned. It has been a part of our lives for as long as we can remember. Sometimes we are not even aware of how changed we really are. We are often not aware of the great power the gospel has been in our lives. For us to see the power of God, we must see it at work in the lives of others. To see it at work in the lives of others, we must step out in faith believing what Paul said about the gospel, "It is the power of God for salvation to everyone who believes . . ." (Rom. 1:16).

I have often been thrilled by the story of David and Goliath, when David went out against this giant, it required a step of faith. Yes, he had "killed both the lion and the bear," but Goliath was neither a lion nor a bear. Goliath was a huge man who frightened the whole army of Israel.

David went out against this man with two thoughts in mind. Goliath had ridiculed the "armies of the living God," and David believed God to be on his side. He said to the giant, "You come to me with a sword, a spear, and a javelin, but I come to you in the name of the Lord of hosts, the God of the armies of Israel, whom you have taunted . . . ." (1 Sam. 17). He went out with a sling and some stones. Goliath, armed with sword, spear, and javelin, thought David was just a foolish kid. But one stone thrown in the name of the Lord is more powerful than any weapon man could devise and use in his own strength. David took a step of faith, went out in the name of the Lord, and won a great victory.

Similar victories will be ours if we step out in faith, armed with the gospel; telling the good news in the name of the Lord. Many youth and adults have come alive as they became involved in this step of faith. Greater spiritual growth is seen in people who witness than in any other activity. First, they witness first hand what God can do. As they go out in the name of Jesus to proclaim the gospel, they see doors opening, and people willingly receiving them and listening to the gospel. They come to know that God does work miracles as they do His work. They are even amazed at what they are able to do and to say. A young man on the way home from a weekend of witnessing said, "I can't believe I was doing what I was doing." He was overwhelmed by the many people who did not know Jesus as Savior. He found it hard to believe that he had been telling people, "Jesus has lived, died, and rose again for your sins."

Secondly, people who witness grow more rapidly than other Christians because of the power of the Gospel. Most generally, in a training program of three months or more, a person has the opportunity to see someone receive Christ as their Savior. This has an impact upon those who are making the call. On one occasion, it seemed that the Holy Spirit was especially blessing our efforts. Three people, hearing the gospel, invited Christ into their lives. The three of us who were making the visit had more than a couple of tears in our eyes. God had overcome every obstacle, and had prepared their hearts for a moving reception of the gospel.

Thirdly, people who witness grow more rapidly than other Christians because they hear the gospel more often. One course at the Seminary taught me only one thing, but what I learned has been of tremendous value to me. What I learned was this: Faith is created and faith grows only through the hearing of the gospel. Faith cannot be created without the gospel and faith cannot grow without the gospel. If this is true, and I believe it is, then those who hear the gospel the most, under the influence of the Holy Spirit, will have the greatest growth in faith. Those who witness are constantly involved with the gospel. If they are accompanying someone else, they hear him speak the gospel. If they are doing the speaking, they hear themselves speak the gospel. The Holy Spirit works mightily in us through the gospel whether it is spoken by us or someone else.

Most Christians do not witness because they are not willing to go "out on a limb" for the Lord. They can know the gospel, they can know how to speak the gospel, and yet not go out. I believe it is possible for Christians to learn a method of evangelism on their own, to go out on their own, and to know the Lord is with them all the way. But since most Christians are not doing this, it becomes necessary for someone to take others "out on the limb." They need to see that it is safe out there. It is there where we see the miracles of God and the effectiveness of the gospel as it is simply spoken. We need to take fellow Christians "out on the limb," to teach people how to witness, to give them on the job training.

Witnessing is like going out on a limb because there are many indefinite things involved. Will we be rudely treated at the door, or graciously received? To whom will we be speaking? What kind of a person will he be? What will the situation be like? Will the television be on? Will children be running wild? Will this household have visitors? What will be their response? How will we be treated? Will we be ridiculed? The truth is: We do not know what to expect when we knock on a door. For example, we knocked on one door only to discover that they had visitors. We said, "We didn't realize you had visitors. Could we come another time?" I would rather have come another time, but this party invited us in. This is awkward for me for as I present the gospel, I want to give them an opportunity to invite Christ into their lives. With others present, some will accept or reject the invitation to receive Christ because of embarrassment. My first thought was to have a friendly visit, invite them to church, leave, and come another time. As we were talking, we discovered that the man of the house was soon to leave for Vietnam. Then I knew the Lord wanted us there. I presented the gospel, and felt uneasy again when it came time for the commitment question. However, I was pushed on by the thought that this man was soon to leave and probably I would never see him again. So I asked them if they would like to receive Christ, and they both answered yes. After leading them in prayer, I said a special prayer asking God's blessings upon them then and when they would be separated. We left the house feeling we had been where God wanted us to be. I had ignored the visiting couple because of the situation as it was. Later, I learned that those who had been visiting in the home were happy we had come and were thankful for what we had done. This is just one example of how the Lord moves in mysterious and wonderful ways as we go out in His name. We learn as we do His work that what appears to be going out on a limb is really walking on the solid rock of His promises.

In this book, we are concerned with the question, "Where has all the power gone?" I am convinced that while many of our people are prepared for the war, very few ever get involved in the battle. We are witnessing little of the power of God today because little power is being unleashed upon the world by a proclamation of the gospel. We are thankful for the proclamation of the gospel in our pulpits. We need to take this gospel out into the market places of life and into the homes of those who might never come into the house of God. One church ends its bulletin each Sunday with the words: "The worship is over—the service now begins." We need to be fortified by the word we hear so we might be able to break through the fortifications that surround every human life. We can share the gospel we hear with others, and we need to see this as a necessity. I have heard some relaying a story or a joke from a sermon but who never got to the point of why the story or joke was told. I have never heard anyone share the gospel they heard from a sermon on Sunday morning.

So few are proclaiming the gospel. We have called just about everything church work. We can work many hours planning bake sales, smorgasbords, and rummage sales. Some even get very upset when others are not involved as they are. One would think that these things are the kingdom's first concern. Yet we see no command from the Lord, no example from the early church, to give us the idea that we should be doing these things today. The main reason for having them is to raise money. However, if all the people who are involved in these projects would put forth the same time and effort in learning to witness and then in witnessing, money would never be a problem. In themselves, these things are not wrong. They become wrong when they are made to appear as more important than the great commission. Another reason given for having these activities in the church is fellowship. It is admitted that there is always fellowship as Christians work or even play together.

No fellowship, however, can match the fellowship of those whose primary work is to witness. No fellowship can match that of those coming back from witnessing either with battle fatigue or with the spoils of victory. There is no closer fellowship because they gather in the name of Jesus, pray in His name for blessings, witness of Him, and praise Him for all He has done for them. We will have a different feeling toward others after we become involved with them in this spiritual dimension. We will never be moved by the fellowship of a rummage sale as we will by the fellowship of evangelists.

Some church work is only an excuse for not doing what our Lord has told us to do. If we are not carrying out the command of the Lord in one area, we will invent something else so we can feel we are doing some work for the Lord. Many of the things we call church work today could be turned over to atheists and have it done just as well.

We know what our work is to be, but we are kept from it for a number of reasons. Fear, no doubt, more than anything else, keeps us from witnessing. There is the fear of embarrassment, the fear of being thought of as a fanatic, the fear of not doing it well enough, and perhaps even a fear of physical harm. But God has promised to be with us. He has said, "I will never desert you, nor will I ever forsake you" (Heb. 13:5). After Jesus said, "All authority has been given to Me in heaven and on earth . . ." He gave the great commission, and then said, "Lo, I am with you always, even to the end of the age" (Matt. 28:18-20). We are given words of comfort when we seemingly go out on a limb for the Lord. "Who . . . walks in darkness and has no light? Let him trust in the name of the Lord and rely on his God" (Is. 49:10). God uplifts us by His words: "Do not fear, for I have redeemed you; I have called you by name; you are mine! When you pass through the waters, I will be with you; and through the rivers, they will not overflow you. When you walk through the fire, you will not be scorched, nor will the flame burn you. For I am the Lord your God, the Holy One of Israel, your Savior . . ." (Is. 43:1-3). The promise of Jesus, which should not exclude preparation on our part, is most certainly true. "The Holy Spirit will teach you in that very hour what you ought to say" (Luke 12:12). Many have experienced the fulfillment of this promise in their own lives.

"Out on a limb" is intended to mean that we are willing to do something simply because the Lord has commanded it and because he has promised to be with us as we do it. God's command plus His promise means that I must step out in faith before I can experience the reality of His presence in the situation. We do, however, need some kind of plan or method to follow. The professor of evangelism at the Seminary told us to write a witness essay. We were to memorize it and repeat it each time we witnessed for our Savior. I never did use the message I wrote at that time. What I did learn was the importance of developing a witness message. This method assures you of having something to say without leaving crucial points out. This kind of witnessing can sound canned. It will not be if we will trust the Lord to use us, remain calm as we speak, and present the message slowly and clearly. It helps to remember that it is probably the first time for the one who is hearing it. With a memorized message, you can add or take away the frills without discarding the essential part of your witness.

This book is not intended to give a witness message. You can learn a message, and develop your own message from other books. The main issues are the law and the gospel. People must understand, according to the law, we are all lost and condemned sinners in the sight of God. They must understand, according to the gospel, Jesus satisfied divine justice by suffering and dying for our sins. We can speak of Christ's resurrection as proof of God's forgiveness, and of His ascension as the time when He was seated on His throne to rule the world. We need to speak of man's need to trust in Jesus Christ alone for salvation—that all of man's efforts to save himself are futile—and that assurance of salvation comes to us as we trust the promises of God. Once our message is ready, we must go out fortified with the Word of God and prayer.

There is an incentive for witnessing when we realize there are many things which most people do not know about Christianity. They can know many things without knowing the most crucial things. We must witness especially concerning those things that they do not know. God can be thought of as a loving God, and because of His love, He will simply overlook sins. When one man was asked the question, "Why do you expect to go to heaven?" he answered, "Because God forgives." We may think this answer is good; but there can be a number of wrong reasons why people think God forgives. So I ask this man another question, "Can you give me a reason why God should forgive your sins?" Instead of pointing to the cross, the only reason for our forgiveness, he began to talk about his works, treating his neighbor right, etc. Many people believe that God forgives because they are good; but if they are good, there is no need for forgiveness. Forgiveness comes with the confession of sins and not with the confession of good works.

The following list will give you some idea of what most people do not know: Salvation is a free gift earned by Christ for all men, works have no value in obtaining eternal life, God demands payment for sins committed, God has exacted payment for all sin from His only begotten Son, salvation must be received and can only be received by faith, eternal life is ours when we trust in Jesus Christ alone to save us, our works are our thank offerings to God for His goodness, and we can be sure we are going to heaven when we die. What they do not know, we must tell them.

It is a good practice to have a word of prayer before making visits. We should ask the Lord to guide us to the home where He Himself would come. We should ask Him for courage to speak and to lead us to speak the right thing at the right time. We should end by placing ourselves into His hands for Him to use. When we do this, we have the assurance that whether we see victory or apparent defeat, we are doing what our Savior wanted us to do.

Before the proclamation of the gospel can become a natural part of our everyday life, we need to practice it wherever we might be. We need to have the name of Jesus often on our lips. We need to share the gospel in our church meetings, Bible classes, and fellowship meetings. We need to hear the message of the gospel in our homes. In most homes, children hear the law 99percent of the time. Perhaps 1 percent of the time, they hear the gospel if that often. The law is not the power of God to change lives or to strengthen faith. The law by itself is destructive leading to despair and can even lead our children to think that they are not the children of God. If parents would remember, that every time they correct their children for wrongdoing, to tell them of God's love and forgiveness, God's power would be felt in our homes. The law indeed has a power; but it is a power to convict and to condemn. The law is needed, but only to pave the way for an eager reception of the good news. Sometime, at a devotion with your children, say, "I have scolded you many times for the things you did wrong today. I want you to know that Jesus has died for those wrongs. God will forgive you if you will confess your wrong and believe that Jesus has died for you."

If we put ourselves to the task of witnessing, we will find all other activities in the church more meaningful. You will not be selfishly thinking about yourself, but you will be thinking about people who do not know Christ. You will discover many people who have never heard the real gospel. Many times people have said to me, "This is the first time I have ever heard of salvation being a free gift."

The study of the Word of God will become more meaningful as the promises of God come alive as you take your stand on them. Prayer will have a bigger part in your life as you intercede for those who have recently accepted the gospel, and even for some who reject it. It is a whole new world for those who come to know Christ for the first time. "If any man is in Christ, he is a new creature; the old things passed away; behold, new things have come" (2 Cor. 5:17). It is also a whole new world for the Christian who goes from and in his believing to witnessing for his Savior. It is a whole new world of rejoicing as we at times "suffer shame for His name" (Acts 5:41), but also a whole new world of rejoicing over the lost sheep that is found and over the one sinner who repents (Luke 15:6-7).

All the joy we get from witnessing will make worthwhile all the efforts we put into learning how to do it. A young girl, who was with me making calls on an OAFC weekend, had a difficult time holding back the tears as we were witnessing. She herself, in these calls, was discovering or rediscovering the Savior who loved her very much. I can remember the joy I felt when this young lady went on to be one of the better members of the Ongoing Ambassador for Christ program. You find joy in witnessing as the early disciples did, but your greatest joy should always be as Jesus said, "Rejoice that your names are recorded in heaven" (Luke 10:20). This makes better witnesses than anything else.

Anyone who has it in his heart can witness. If you are willing to risk a little embarrassment as you fumble around for words, if you are willing to give up a little time for God's Word, for prayer, and for practice, you can become a witness. Keep in mind that God is happy with our first foolish attempts. Certainly, we want to work to perfect our witness, but God, by no means, wants us to be silent until we are perfect, or else, no witnessing would be done. Remember, a feeble, faltering witness is better than no witness at all.

I do believe we need to ask for a commitment after our gospel presentation. For many years, I spoke the gospel without ever asking if people wanted what God was offering to them. I will never forget the first time I asked a man if he would like to invite Christ into his life. He was eighty years old, living alone in his house two blocks from church, and not attending any church. This also was the first time I had taken anyone with me on an evangelism call. After presenting the gospel, I asked if he would like to receive Christ into his life. I just about fell off my chair when he said he would. All three of us who had called on him went back to the church rejoicing over an experience we had never had before.

Our church hesitates some to encourage people to ask for a commitment. It bothered me at first because it appeared we would be promoting work righteousness. Some do say, "You take the first step, and God will do the rest." Passages like Romans 10:20, "I was found by those who did not seek Me, I became manifest to those who did not ask for me" have led us to believe that all the steps taken, were taken by God and not by us. It is grace all the way. However, I do not think we will have any problems with the prayer of commitment if we put it into the hands of the Holy Spirit as well as the presentation of the gospel. We leave it in the hands of the Holy Spirit whether or not faith is created; whether or not a prayer is to be said. If faith has been awakened in the heart, the prayer of commitment becomes a prayer of confession as to what has happened. Perhaps there can be a prayer of commitment spoken without faith. It would be done by some people who want to do everything that sounds religious. The Pharisees did something like this when they came to John the Baptist wanting to be baptized without any change of heart. Such a prayer, however, would be of no value to anyone.

The percentage of those who witness is so small compared with the large number who have never tried it, or who have tried it and never did again. Where has all the power gone? To the same place where our witnessing has gone. The power of the early church will return to us only as the witnessing of the early church returns. The only way it will return is when it becomes the main subject of our study and conversation. We need to talk about witnessing in our Bible Studies, Ladies' meetings, Men's meetings, until the message is obvious: "We are less than what we should be as a church until witnessing becomes our way of life."

After having gone through two Bible studies which were telling us how to witness, one lady said, "We are always hearing about witnessing from the pulpit, and now again in these Bible Studies. I really want to, but I still don't know how." Needless to say, she was the first to be asked to be a part of an evangelism training program. Both she and her husband became evangelists. When God's people have an earnest desire to do His will, and His will is sought by the Word of God and prayer, it will come to pass. If we will go out on a limb for the Savior, witnessing without knowing what the results will be, we will see good things—the sure hand of God with us and His power flowing to us and through us to others,

> Send Thou, O Lord, to ev'ry place
> Swift messengers before Thy face,
> The heralds of Thy wondrous grace,
> Where Thou Thyself wilt come.
>
> Raise up, O Lord the Holy Ghost,
> From this broad land a mighty host;
> Their war cry, "We will seek the lost
> Where Thou, O Christ, wilt come." TLH 506

Chapter 9

In His Hands

POWER FROM THE Lord is lost in the church because of a lack of trust in the Lord. This lack of trust in the Lord is often seen in the form of frustration, anger, fear, doubt and pessimism. In so many incidences of our lives, we fail to place ourselves and our situations in God's hands. In both Luther's morning and evening prayers, he prayed: "For into Your hands I commend myself, my body and soul, and all things." Putting ourselves and our situations in God's hands would help us feel better as individuals and would be a great blessing to the church. It involves the matter of knowing when we should be doing something and of knowing when only God is able to act in our behalf. It involves trusting the Lord for guidance, for security, and in circumstances when our finite wisdom cannot know why something is happening as it is.

Our lack of trust and our failure toward commitment comes from our lack of knowledge concerning the Lord. The greatest challenge in our lives is to know the Lord and all about Him. The more we know about God, the more we know of His love and concern, the more we will trust Him and place ourselves in His hands. The Psalmist said, "O taste and see that the Lord is good . . ." (Ps. 34:8). People who are constantly grumbling and complaining are not showing their appreciation for all that God stands for. They do not show their appreciation of all that it means to be a child of God.

Perhaps it is like my family's interest in the Night Blooming Primrose. A friend invited us to see this amazing plant. We liked what we saw so much that we were thrilled when another friend gave us some plants to set out. The plant produces a number of stems and on each stem it produces a number of buds. The outer buds grow most rapidly. When they are the right size, during the afternoon and early evening, the green calyx splits and then waits until it is almost dark. At a certain time, the sepals pull back and the bud bursts open into a beautiful yellow flower. This latter sequence takes place in a matter of seconds. The flowers bloom all night and then wither during the next day. By the next evening, another group of buds are ready to put on their show. My family and I were awed by this miracle of God. But after we had watched these night after night in our own yard, they soon lost their attraction. Now, they burst into bloom almost unnoticed. The miracle is as great as ever, but we no longer see it as of any great interest.

So, for many, the basics of Christianity have lost their exciting luster. It no longer seems a miracle to be a Christian—to know God loves you and forgives you for Jesus' sake—and to know that God cares about you and sustains you every minute of every day. God hasn't changed but perhaps our appreciation of Him has.

In our day, many nondenominational churches have formed. In most cases, these churches come into existence because some aspect of Christianity is not being practiced by the main line churches. Some are formed around the theme of praising the Lord. Another group forms expressing a need for greater spirituality—to experience power rather than just talking about it. Often their main theme is dealing with the miraculous; healing and other gifts of the Spirit. Some emphasize the need for self-surrender to the Lord. While we need to be aware of the dangers involved in many movements of today, we need to be listening to them because some express what we of the main line churches are not practicing to any noticeable degree. The danger of some of these groups is that their main theme will overshadow the central theme of Christianity which is that we are justified by grace through faith in

Jesus Christ without the deeds of the law. But while it may happen that the emphasis of some tends to obscure the central teaching of Christianity, we may have to admit that what they emphasize is often omitted or given little attention in our own circles.

The main line churches are sometimes chided for their lack of commitment to the Lord Jesus. They say, "What you need to do is to surrender your life to the Lord." While this is true, they often offer more because of the surrender than is scripturally warranted. The receiving of things is based on your giving of yourself so that your gift is not based on grace but upon works. Because of some false premises, some accept Christianity in the wrong way. If, for example, a person believes his troubles will all end if he gives his life to Jesus, he will be in for a surprise and his faith will be in for a shock. St. Paul in strengthening the churches of his day said,

"Through many tribulations we must enter the kingdom of God" (Acts 14:22).

But even though some of these movements may be wrong in the way they sell the idea of surrender, they are right in saying we need to surrender our lives to the Lord. In this chapter, "In His Hands" means that. In so many ways, we need to say to each other in the church where we belong, "Commit your way to the Lord, Trust also in Him, and He will do it" (Ps. 37:5).

We need to put ourselves into the hands of the Lord for Him to use. We need to trust Him for His guidance. We should seek the Lord's Will in every situation. The first source, and the only sure source, for God's direction is His Word as we find it in the Bible. You cannot be absolutely certain of God's direction in any other way. He has given us rules by which we are to govern our lives. We cannot come to any conclusion which would lead us to go contrary to any Word which He has given us. When some operate on the principle, "the end justifies the means," they will find themselves often living contrary to the Will of God and in reality, taking their lives and the situation into their own hands. An extreme example of how wrong that principle can be is to imagine a woman becoming a prostitute in order to give greater contributions to the church.

There are situations where an answer from the Bible cannot be found. For some of these, we may find it helpful to ask, "What would Jesus do?" or better, "What does Jesus want me to do?" This question helps us to clarify our thinking; but even when we do this and add a prayer to it, we may still make a wrong decision. Sometimes we simply have to say, "Lord, I believe this is what you want me to do. If I am wrong, show me, and correct the mistake." Trust the Lord. Place yourself into His hands as you do what you planned.

Many today are saying and many are led to believe that God gives them direct guidance. We hear it said on television that the Lord speaks to us in so many wonderful ways—through dreams, visions, miracles, an inner voice, and also through the Word. All except the last must be seen as perhaps helpful but never as the final word in any decision. We know these things happened in Biblical times. But most of these happened because they did not have a completed Bible as we do today. How would they know what to believe if God did not talk to them directly? Revelation had to be given, but now that it has been given, we cannot be certain of receiving any more. If you believe that God speaks today through dreams, visions, miracles, and the inner voice, you will be subject to follow any man who claims to have these experiences. The Mormons and the Jehovah's Witnesses are good examples of people who have followed men who claimed these things for themselves. If a person has an experience, it may prove helpful to him but it is of no benefit to me because there is no way I can verify its occurrence or the truthfulness of it.

One must even question his own experiences. Those who say, "A voice came to me," still must question where the voice came from. Satan spoke to Eve in the garden of Eden. He spoke to Jesus in the wilderness to tempt Him. He must have spoken through Peter because Jesus said to him, "Get behind Me, Satan!" (Matt. 16:23). And how do we know that the voice is not our own reason which is finite and warped by sin? We must remember "Satan disguises himself as an angel of light" (2 Cor. 11:14). The Bible speaks of "the one whose coming is in accord with the activity of Satan, with all power and signs and false wonders" (2 Thess. 2:10). Those who will be deceived will be those who do not love the truth—that is, the bare Word as we have it in the Bible (v.11). We must always be aware of the deception that can come to us through visions, dreams, voices, miracles, and other experiences. They must be tested in every way through the Word given by the Holy Spirit in the Bible.

There are those who seem to stay alive on the basis of the experiences of others. They have never had an experience themselves but they are always running after others who make these claims. So we have auditoriums filled with people who go to see the wonder workers. They give the impression that they are very much spiritually alive as they tell of the wonders of those they hear. Yet many of these do not speak of their joy which results from their own relationship with Jesus Christ. It is as if they derive their strength from what they hear is happening to others, and live in anxious anticipation of having an experience similar to those they hear.

Then there are those who seek signs for guidance in an imitation of Gideon and his fleece. (Judges 6). We are led to ask, "Are the signs today similar to Gideon's where he not only ask for one sign but for a second for verification?" "Is the sign truly miraculous or is it something like saying, 'If the sun is shining in the morning, this will be a sign for us to undertake the project?'" Without asking any questions like these, many expect God to hand them everything they need as if all they have to do is snap their fingers and God goes to work for them. They can give the impression that you do not have to work, think or plan. All you have to do is pray enough and believe enough and you will ride along on the crest of the wave of God's constant care. God has created man to rule over His creation and has created him with the ability to do so. And God expects man to work as we are told, "If anyone is not willing to work, then he is not to eat, either" (2 Thess. 3:10).

Christians need to think and work. They need to use the strength and the brains God gives them.

Let us look at the elements of truth many of these proclaim but let us make sure they are not saying too much. We must trust God to guide us. We may have swung to the other side of the pendulum and say that God never gives guidance apart from the Word. But anyone who has been involved in Evangelism expects God to guide him to the home where God wants him to be. We pray to God and trust Him to lead us to the homes where He Himself would come. We believe God has led us to homes whether the door was slammed in our face or we and the Gospel were received warmly. Day by day, we are to put ourselves into the hands of God so He will lead us to those people who need a Word of comfort or a deed of kindness. We pray for God's guidance in the Voters' Assembly. We pray for the outcome of a vote. We pray for God to lead others to our place of worship and we expect God, in some ways, to begin His work directly upon them. We can believe that even before we pray for someone, God has already begun His work to prepare the heart for a reception of our spoken Word.

We can benefit greatly if we trust God's guidance in every situation. So much of the anger we experience is due to our unwillingness to rest our case with God. We go to a meeting with our minds set as to the outcome. We are so convinced we are right. We will fight anyone to whatever extent to get our own way. But when we do not, we become depressed, angry, frustrated, and revengeful; and this hurts us more than anyone else. These should be signs to us that we are taking too much into our own hands. There is a better way. Before any meeting in the church or with people elsewhere, sit down and spend some time with God. Read at least one chapter of the Bible, pray for what you believe is right, and ask God to be with you to bring a blessing to the meeting. Then go and defend your idea to the best of your ability but leave the outcome to God. If it goes against your way, do not blame yourself or others. Simply let it rest with God. Place yourself, others, and the situation in God's hands before, during and after any circumstance with which you must deal. This will eliminate much of the frustration and anger experienced in life. We must simply learn when we must do something and when we must let God. When we do not know when to let go and let God, we burden ourselves unnecessarily. Peter wrote, "Casting all your anxiety upon Him, because He cares for you" (1 Peter 5:7).

We must place our church growth in the hands of God. It can be a frustrating experience for pastors and people when the attendance is low in church and when there is a lack of growth. Our concern should be with doing the work which the Lord has given us to do.

We are to be busy with things pertaining to the Word and Sacrament. We are to baptize. We are to make the Lord's Supper available to God's people. We are to share the Word of God in our own circle as well as out of it. We are to teach, preach, and speak the Word, especially the Word of the Gospel. We have so little confidence in the Gospel. We must believe in its power. If you have to see the power, then you will be like those who tried it once and since nothing happened, they never try it again. Even congregations have judged the power of the Gospel on the basis of growth. They have tried to share the Gospel through programs of Evangelism, but when they realized little or no growth, they gave up. Our use of the Gospel should not be based on whether or not it causes growth. For while the preaching of Christ crucified is a stumbling block to some and foolishness to others, "to those who are the called, both Jews and Greeks," the preaching of Christ is "the power and the wisdom of God" (1 Cor. 1:24-25).

We should pray for the Lord to bless our efforts but the outcome must be left in His hands. We can set goals of how many new members we hope to have and of how many people we want to attend Church on Sunday morning. If we do set goals, we must work and pray to reach the goals, but again, we must leave the results to God. It is frustrating for us if we think we must convert people. It is frustrating because only God can convert and change a human heart. We must rather concentrate on doing our work—proclaiming the Gospel—and trust

God to do His work. We should be active in inviting people to come to church and we should be friendly toward all those who do come; but finally we must trust God to bring them in and to keep them in. Leave the results, whatever they may be, in God's hands.

In a similar way, we need to place ourselves in God's hands for security. We experience worry, fear, and doubt because we do not trust God to protect us and to care for all the bodily needs we experience. But why do we not trust God? It is because we know we are not perfect human beings. We have lived our lives contrary to the Word of God. We know deep down in our hearts we are not what we should be and are deserving of punishment. We know how people of this world have treated us after we have wronged them and so we doubt. But God is different! God is love! God cares about us more than anyone else in this world can care. To see this, we must go to the Cross. At the cross, we see God's love and forgiveness, and because of this, we can believe that every promise of God is intended for us. From the Bible we learn we are God's children through faith in Jesus Christ. From the Bible, we learn that God wants to and knows how to take care of His children in the world. As children of God we can say, "This is my Father's world and He will use the world for my benefit as well as for the benefit of other Christians." Meditate on this passage: "He who did not spare His Son, but delivered Him up for us all, how will He not also with Him freely give us all things?" (Rom. 8:32). Believe on the basis of Jesus' Words: "Do not be anxious then, saying, 'What shall we eat?' or 'What shall we drink?' or 'With what shall we clothe ourselves?' For the Gentiles eagerly seek all these things; for your Heavenly Father knows that you need all these things" (Matt. 6:31-32). There are other passages of the Bible telling us of God's protection and of His angels' activities in our behalf. We must believe that God is watching out for our welfare and we should trust His desire to help and His ability to help in every situation.

You cannot, however, be living contrary to God's commands and expect everything to turn out right. The man who takes his paycheck and throws it all away in a tavern the first night cannot expect God to take care of his daily needs. The highly spiritual person who prays every day for God to take care of his physical needs cannot expect God to answer his prayer if he is not willing to work. The teenager who drives his car 90 mph around a sharp curve cannot expect the angels to keep his car on the road. The same is true for those who ignore the warnings of the Bible about false teachings. Claiming to be able to sift the good from the bad, many listen to every preacher they hear on radio and television. Ignoring God's directives, they take their faith in their own hands. We cannot ignore the guidelines God has given us and expect His promises to be applicable to our situation.

But we live under the umbrella of God's grace and forgiveness as we daily repent of our sins and believe Jesus has died for them. As we live with repentant hearts, we can believe all the promises God has given. Even if we have sinned and gone astray, we can turn to the Lord and trust Him to give us guidance and show us the right way back. At any time, when we place ourselves in His hands, God will go to work in our behalf. No matter how difficult it is to come out of the situation, God will be with us every step of the way. He will reach down, lift up, and restore us as we turn to Him as children would turn to a loving father.

We can worry about our children. We can fear for the well-being of relatives and friends in a foreign country where war has broken out. In so many situations, we find there is nothing at the moment we can do and we must place our loved ones, our problems, in God's hands. Because this is not easy to do, we need our Bibles. When worry and fear enter our hearts, we need to turn to God's Word, read it, and then pray for whatever bothers us. Turn it over to the Lord and leave it there. God knows how to take care of every situation.

This, in no way, gives us an excuse for being lazy. If there is something we can do, we should do it; but when there is nothing more we can do, trust God to act in our behalf and in our best interest. "Trust in the Lord with all your heart, and do not lean on your own understanding" (Prov. 3:5). God will never let you down. This is difficult to believe at times, but we must persist in our belief because it is true.

Confirmation is to be the time when we knowledgeably give our lives to the Lord. We can call it surrender, a yielding, or a commitment. Jesus expects His followers to be committed. Paul expected this from the people of Rome. He wrote, "I urge you, brethren, by the mercies of God, to present your bodies a living and holy sacrifice, acceptable to God, which is your spiritual service of worship" (Romans 12:1). It seems that surrendering to the Lord was intended to bring about harmony among the members of the church at Rome. If we do not permit God to rule our lives in the church, tyrants will. So Paul calls on people to "be transformed" rather than "conformed to this world." He warns against thinking too highly of ourselves and tells us to through the yielding of ourselves to the Lord to discover what the will of God is. In verses 9 through 21, Paul gives a splendid code of ethics for us to use in our daily lives and to follow in all our church activities.

There are those who would encourage us to surrender ourselves totally and completely to God. We should do this; but we must be aware of the impossibility of any human being accomplishing this. Only Jesus, God's Son, could and did surrender Himself completely to do the will of His Heavenly Father. But because we cannot do it perfectly, it does not mean we should do nothing. As the Holy Spirit moves us through the Word and Sacrament, we need to yield more and more of ourselves to God.

Without trying to be judgmental, it seems we would find only 25 to 30 percent of the members of our churches being involved. Some of these become involved too much and neglect their homes and families. Every Christian should be committed to some activity in the church for the sake of Christ and His kingdom. One person may be involved in the choir. He needs to be committed to the choir and to be there for every practice. Another one may choose to be in the Evangelism program. He needs to be committed to weekly meetings and visitations. One night a week is not too much to ask of those who sing: "Take my life and let it be Consecrated, Lord, to Thee." If every Christian would make such a commitment, it would make it possible for other members to spend more nights at home with their families.

But we ask the question, "Where has all the power gone?" If we would place ourselves in the hands of God by simple trust, this would keep our failures from eating away at our inner strength. We waste our strength by trying to do those things which only God can do. We preserve our strength for other things when we let God do His work. We use the power which God gives through His Word and Sacrament when we become involved in some activity for Christ and His Church in the world. We can say we are unleashing the power of God into the world as we are activated through the Word of God that has come into our lives. In some cases, the power of Christ is never used. So the power within us becomes available to the world, we must pray, "Use me Lord; I place the members of my body in Your service." When the Lord wants to use us, we should be available and ready.

There is one more area, at least, where we need to place ourselves in God's hands and trust Him completely. This is in suffering. Those who advocate praising God for everything, tell us to praise God for a flat tire as well as for a safe trip without one and to praise God for sickness as well as for health. It is a Biblical thought which we should accept and practice. We may fail to put this thought to use in our lives simply because another group has suggested and practices it. So if Baptists say, "Praise God," or the Charismatics say, "Praise God," should this keep us from saying it when we feel like it and mean it? It would not be proper to praise God for the evil we do or for the evil others have done, but we can praise God for the good He brings out of evil. God brought good out of the evil thoughts and actions of Joseph's brothers not only for the good of Joseph but also for his father, brothers, and for a multitude of people of his day. Joseph said to his brothers, "You meant evil against me, but God meant it for good in order to bring about this present result, to preserve many people alive" (Gen. 50:20). What we enjoy in life comes from a loving God, but also what we suffer comes from a loving God, and this suffering is intended for our good.

In the hymn, "Why should cross and trial grieve me?" (TLH 523), we see two verses especially speaking to this point. They are:

Though a heavy cross I'm bearing, and my heart feels the smart. Shall I be despairing? God, my helper, who doth send it, well both know all my woe and how best to end it.

God oft gives me days of gladness; shall I grieve if He give seasons, too, of sadness? God is good and tempers ever, all my ill, and he will wholly leave me never.

We can be thankful to the Lord for suffering; we can praise Him for it because we know God intends it for our good. "Praise to God" is so often absent from our lips because we do not trust God in every situation. We may believe things to be out of His hands. As a result, our lives are often filled with gloom. However, there are many places in the Bible which tell us that our lives should be filled with joy and praise. "Be filled with the Spirit, speaking to one another in psalms and hymns and spiritual songs, singing and making melody with your heart to the Lord; always giving thanks for all things in the name of our Lord Jesus Christ to God, even the Father" (Eph. 5:18-20). The advice given to the Ephesians by Paul was given also to the people of Thessalonica. "Rejoice always; pray without ceasing; in everything give thanks; for this is God's will for you in Christ Jesus" (1 Thess. 5:16-18).

Suffering is not an experimental program. It involves all the knowledge and wisdom of a loving God who knows best what is good for us. When suffering comes our way, we often ask, "Why, Lord? Why me?" While we cannot always know the specific reason, we can know the general principle which stands behind it all. God wants to make us better people. The Lord purifies and changes His people through persecution, and if not by persecution, then by the suffering common to all men. At times, we may wonder why God's people seem to suffer more than the non-Christian; but the Bible says, "For those whom the Lord loves He disciplines, And He scourges every Son whom He receives" (Heb. 12:6). God wants to give us something better than what non-Christians experience. He wants to give us real joy rather than the often synthetic joy of the world. He wants to give us a more settled peace. We have a tendency to believe that joy comes through possessing and using the material things of the world. We may believe we would have joy if we had a new home, lived in a crime-free society, and dealt only with loveable and likeable people. But God's joy is deeper than this. God's joy is something we can experience without having any of these things. It amazes us at times to see people being joyful when they have to bear a very difficult hardship.

Suffering, however, to be beneficial, must be accepted. Too many Christians groan and complain about their misfortunes, and the very thing intended to help them turns out to be harmful. Instead of becoming better, they become bitter. On the other hand, suffering will be beneficial if it is accepted as coming from the good and loving hand of God. To help us accept our suffering, we need to read passages from the Bible like the one Paul wrote to the Philippians. "Rejoice in the Lord always; again I will say, rejoice! Let your forbearing spirit be known to all men. The Lord is near. Be anxious for nothing, but in everything by prayer and supplication with thanksgiving let your requests be made known to God. And the peace of God, which surpasses all comprehension, shall guard your hearts and your minds in Christ Jesus" (Phil. 4:4-7).

We seldom know the specific reason for an individual's suffering. Assuming what it might be is dangerous. We must simply see suffering as being used by God to bring about good for the individual and for the world. All that a Christian suffers will eventually come to an end. Perhaps we need to admit the need for suffering now so we will be saved for heaven where we will never have to suffer again.

I knew a family who had to endure a severe trial of faith. A teenage son had been hit by a car. He was taken to a hospital where he was in a coma for a long period of time. They were told by the doctor that he was not expected to live and if he did, he would be a vegetable. They continued to pray day after day until finally he regained consciousness. He recovered to the extent of being able to talk a little and to move a little; but he was never to progress beyond the wheel chair. I counseled the parents by simply saying, "God loves you, and intends to bring some good out of this for yourselves and for those around you." They accepted this remarkably well.

I also ministered to the boy. He was given over into deep depression. He had been very athletic, but now he was confined to the bed and only occasionally to sit in a wheel chair. In his case, the joy of heaven became more meaningful. It is said that the youth of our day do not want a religion offering only "pie in the sky in the sweet by and by." They want religion to offer them something right away. This young man, however, seemed happy to hear of how things were going to be in heaven. One day, I played the guitar and sang songs for him. After each song, he would say, "More." I cannot imagine very many teenagers who would sit still long enough to hear more than one of my songs. I am not putting down youth. I am being modest about my songs. After I had finished singing, we talked about the joys of heaven and of how Jesus made this possible by His death and resurrection. Then I said, "You know, the first time I see you in heaven, I am going to run you a race." He smiled and said in his difficult way, "I'll beatcha." This gives me another reason for looking forward to heaven—the foot race with Danny.

There are those who say you can be healed of anything if you have enough faith. This is not realistic nor is it Biblical. As was said before, suffering involves the wisdom of God who knows what we need to suffer, how much and how long it ought to be. We should pray for what we want whether it be for healing or other material gifts, but faith in the ultimate sense is the ability to place the answer in God's hands and trust that He knows best how to handle it. If a person never carries a burden, never exercises his muscles, his muscles will grow flabby and weak. If we had no suffering and no burdens, we would become spiritual weaklings. This life only involves a short period of time—perhaps seventy or eighty years. Some days may seem like forever but as we place our days in God's hands, they all become a little shorter and a little more joyful as we are drawn a little closer each day to a loving Father. We should agree with Paul who wrote, "I consider that the sufferings of this present time are not worthy to be compared with the glory that is to be revealed to us" (Rom. 8:18). What life we have left we should want to be filled with praise and thanksgiving as we think of all Jesus has done to save us, of all He is doing right now to keep us close to Him, and of all the pleasures He will yet give us as we spend an eternity with Him in heaven.

What a pleasant church it would be if people would decide to stop their griping and complaining and begin to praise God for big things and small things and to thank Him for everything. We need to trust God to take charge of our lives and we need to be joyful every step of the way. This kind of activity speaks a language all its own which says, "There is joy in knowing Jesus. I have joy because I have Jesus the Giver of all good things."

Where has all the power gone? To the same place where our joy, thanksgiving, and praise have gone. When our confidence and trust in God's love and care return, so will the joy. When our joy in the Lord returns, so will the power. In Nehemiah 8:10, we read: "Do not be grieved, for the joy of the Lord is your strength." And so we ought to sing with the Psalmist, "Restore to me the joy of Your salvation . . ." (Ps. 51:12). This joy will be ours more constantly as we by faith place ourselves, our situations, our everything daily in His hands.

> Thy ways, O Lord, with wise design
> Are framed upon Thy throne above,
> And ev'ry dark and bending line
> Meets in the center of Thy love. (TLH 530)

Chapter 10

The Conclusion

Do YOU WANT a stronger faith? Do you want yourself and your church to experience more power? For the church to experience and to exhibit the power of God, we must consistently practice the things God has given us for our spiritual welfare. The following check list may prove helpful for a self-examination helping you to see how well you are doing and if there are any areas where spiritual life could be improved. After each statement, mark either yes or no. Be honest with yourself and with God as you examine your spiritual activity.

Spiritual Activity	Yes	No
The first thought that comes to mind when asked, "What does your church teach?" is: "Christ and Him crucified."	____	____
The first thought that comes to mind when asked, "What is the main teaching of the Bible?" is: "Christ and Him crucified." (x)	____	____
I know if I were to die right now I would go to heaven.	____	____
I believe the Gospel. I place my whole hope for heaven on Jesus Christ and what He has done for me on the cross. (x)	____	____

I believe the Bible is God's inspired and inerrant Word. (x)   _____ _____

The Bible is clear enough for me to understand it.   _____ _____

I hear the Word of God in church nearly every Sunday.(x)   _____ _____

I attend a Bible study nearly every week.   _____ _____

I read my Bible nearly every day.   _____ _____

I often memorize Scripture portions.   _____ _____

I often sib down to meditate on what the Bible is saying and what it means for my life.   _____ _____

I spend some time each day alone with God in prayer.   _____ _____

My family has daily devotions.   _____ _____

I partake of the Lord's Supper at least once a month.(x) _____ _____

I spend some time with God in prayer with one or more of my fellow church members.   _____ _____

I think often of witnessing to others of Jesus' love.(x) _____ _____

I witness for Jesus every opportunity I get.   _____ _____

I seek opportunities to witness for my Savior.   _____ _____

I have surrendered my life to Christ.   _____ _____

Daily, I surrender my life to Christ by placing myself in His hands for Him to use, to care for, and to guide.   _____ _____

For the sake of analysis, score yourself five points for every yes answer. I hope I am proved wrong, but the x's you see behind some statements are those I believe would be given by the *average* church member. If this gives us any kind of true picture, we would see the church operating at 30 percent of its spiritual potential. If you want your faith to grow stronger, you increase the number of your spiritual activities. If we could get each member of a church to increase his spiritual activity by at least one more, we would increase the power of the whole church considerably. Suppose every member in a church would decide to read their Bibles every day when only 30 percent had been doing this before. Think of all the power God would place into that Church. This analysis is not intended to be accurate but only to lead us into some serious thinking about the vitality of our own spiritual life. Some helpful things may be omitted from the list, but this, for some, can be the beginning of an examination of a relationship that one has with God through Jesus Christ.

The problem with most Christians is their laziness about spiritual things. They can be told how to grow spiritually. They can be shown how to have personal, private daily devotions. But many would not give up the time or put forth the effort to adopt such a practice. Lazy Christians are easy targets for those who promise instant power and wisdom. They fall for the line, "I will lay my hands on you and pray for you and you will be filled with the Holy Spirit. You will be filled with power." It is similar to people who do not take the time for a regular breakfast and are content with an "instant" breakfast. It is not difficult to see which would have the more value.

We tend to go for what is easy, less time consuming, and simple. Our lazy nature in spiritual things is born of our old Adam. The way of the cross is not the lazy way. We are expected to take up the cross *daily* and follow Jesus. We must put forth effort and perhaps grow slowly but surely as we daily involve ourselves in the Word of God.

It is like the proverb: "You can lead a horse to water but you cannot make him drink." If someone tells us of his desire for a stronger faith, we do not have a button to push to give him instant power. We can show him the way but if he will not walk in the way, we cannot help him.

When I was at the seminary for only a short time, I had what some might call a religious experience. I became thrilled with Christianity as I never had been before. I saw my sinfulness and that of others more clearly, but I also saw my pardon more clearly in the Savior's death and resurrection. For a long time, I wondered why I had such an experience as this. Why at the seminary and not somewhere else? The reason seems to have been my involvement in the Word—my being saturated with the Word, especially with the Word of the Gospel. I had learned to read my Bible every day. We were studying Luther's Small Catechism again as a part of our training. I attended Chapel twice a day and church every Sunday—hearing the Word and singing my praises to God.

Since leaving the seminary, I have wondered how others could be placed in a similar situation without having to go to the Seminary. The church should be the seminary in our home town. But it takes more than the pastor to make it work. Laymen must see the need they have to be fortified by the Word.

I grew up in a Lutheran Christian home and am thankful for parents who took me to Sunday school and church nearly every Sunday. I was a part of the youth group, known then as the Walther League, and enjoyed our monthly Bible studies. On the basis of my life, I am led to conclude that great things do not happen with such a minimal spiritual diet. We need more than a twenty-minute sermon a week and a thirty-minute Bible study a month, especially for this day in which we are living. It makes you fear for those who seem satisfied with attending church once a month and some even less. We need more and it is obvious we should want more. Our loving Father in heaven has chosen one way to communicate with us. When we realize our Father wants to communicate to us through His Word, our desire for the Word should be constant and endless.

If we seriously involve ourselves with the Word, expecting a blessing to come from the involvement, we will grow. Instant power is not likely, but we will grow. We may not see the growth or feel it, but we must believe it because God promises it. "So shall My word be which goes forth from My mouth; It shall not return to Me empty, without accomplishing what I desire, And without succeeding in the matter for which I sent it" (Is. 55:11).

Saving faith is an instant faith. You cannot be partially a believer no more than a woman can be partially pregnant. When conception takes place in a woman, a living being has come into existence; but this living being will need nourishment for months on the inside and even for years on the outside. In fact, it will always need this nourishment if it is to stay alive. So while saving faith comes in an instant, a moment of God's choosing, faith must continue to grow to maturity and cause the person to become instrumental in the building of God's kingdom. The strong faith is the one which goes through tempests and trials and endures on the basis of the Word of God which is the foundation of our faith and life. A strong faith is not based on our own experiences or on the experiences of others which are here today and gone tomorrow; but it is based on "the living and abiding Word of God." "The Word of the Lord abides forever" (1 Peter 1:23-25).

If we want more power in our lives, we must use the means God has chosen to impart it. The Word is the power. We can speak of Sacrament power. The Sacraments, Baptism, and the Lord's Supper do bestow power on us but they convey it because they are used in connection with the Word—God's command and promise. If there were no command and promise, the sacrament would have no value. If you would smear mud all over your body, or swim across the Mississippi, or climb a mountain, simply because someone told you to receive a blessing in that way, you would be foolish to comply because there is no word of command or promise from God to support such statements. To seek power through means other than those God has given us is both foolish and dangerous. The devil offered Jesus the kingdom without the cross. He offers us fulness of power without the cross and without the Word.

We can speak about witness power. This again is Word power which centers in the proclamation of the Gospel.

We can speak about prayer power. When God answers prayers for physical things, there is no doubt He does this directly. But when people pray for spiritual power, the answer must come through the Word. There are those who pray for a stronger faith but who stay at least five feet away from their Bibles and at least a mile away from the church. The Word of God brings the power. So we pray for workers, teachers, pastors, and evangelists. We pray for God to give boldness to their witness of the Word and pray for doors to human hearts to open to receive the Word.

The power is the Word of God. In the beginning, God said, "Let there be light," and light came to be. Jesus said, "Lazarus, come forth," and a man who was dead came back to life. So God's Word will bring life to our deadness. God reaches down with His Word to lift us up and to restore us in fellowship with Himself. When we believe in the power of the Word, when we believe the Word, live by it and act on it, we will soon see the power of God in our lives and the effect it has on the lives of others. When we all believe this and act upon it, power will return to the church as it was in the days when the church was at its best.

If you are a Christian and you know it, there is no reason why you should not be happy. Do we sometime reveal our belief that a non-Christian life is more pleasant than the life of a Christian? Some people give the impression that being a Christian is a burdensome thing. There are those who give evidence that they envy the man who accepts Christ on his death-bed. You can almost hear them saying, "Why should they have all the fun, and then at the end to have heaven too?" We should rather feel sorry for the man *who* has had to live his life without the promise and presence of God. We sing in one hymn, "I need Thy presence every passing hour." A non-Christian knows of no such presence. Anyone who comes to know Jesus can only be sorry he did not know him sooner. I am grateful to God for bringing me into His kingdom as a little child and for keeping me as His child ever since by Word and Sacrament. One man, who was married at fifty years of age, said his only regret was that he had not married sooner. It is true as another man has sung: "The longer I serve Him, the sweeter He grows."

God's people are those who look to God for guidance and power, seeking these through His Word, and who lift up others who are cast down and broken. When you are built up by the Word, you should dedicate yourself to helping others to be built up. Never be a part of putting another person down or in leading another to doubt the promises of God. There may be times when God's hand of judgment and chastisement rests upon a person. But even when we suspect it or even know it, we must seek to comfort him and help him in every way with his affliction. God knows how much and how far his chastisement must go and He needs no help in administering it.

While we will always be inconsistent in our lives, we call these sins, God has been and will always be consistent in His love and grace. As we grow, we learn more and more about the depravity of man and of the human race and we will come to an even deeper understanding of God's infinite love which is "deeper than the deepest ocean, and wider than the sky." We will learn what God said to be true: "'For the mountains may be removed and the hills may shake, But my lovingkindness will not be removed from you, And my covenant of peace will not be shaken, says the Lord who has compassion on you" (Is. 54:10).

We should be thankful to the Lord for placing us in a church which has remained faithful to His Word. Because of this, we should love this church and pray for even greater blessings upon it. We should not want things which would be contrary to God's Word. We should always want the blessings of God which will be consistent with the doctrine already given to us. The greatest blessing God could give today would be to send us a special measure of His Holy Spirit to lead us into a practice of what is already taught, believed, and confessed in our midst.

On occasion, we sing a song which I believe is inconsistent with our reality. We sing, "I love to tell the story, Of Jesus and His glory, To tell the old, old story, of Jesus and His love." We believe in the practice of telling others about Jesus. We thrill to the beautiful sound of the practice, but we do not practice what we are singing. We sing about loving to tell the story when in reality most of our number do not even like to or try to. Or we may sing, "How Precious is the Book Divine," and spend a lifetime without reading it once from cover to cover.

It is because of our many inconsistent ways that we can be thankful for the sure and consistent love and forgiveness of God which is ours abundantly through Jesus Christ, our Savior. This amazing love of God was shown to me even more clearly one night at a Lenten service. The messages from a filmstrip for our Lenten services had been very pointed. In the last segment shown, I was given another view of the cross I had never considered. We had sung the hymn, "Were you there when they crucified my Lord?" The filmstrip proceeded to put us there, making us to be witnesses who had to decide for or against the crucifixion of Jesus. We were called upon to answer the question, "What shall we do with Jesus?" The crowds had shouted, "Crucify Him! Crucify Him!" What would you have said then to the question of Pilate, knowing all that you know now about sin and death, life and salvation? Would we not have to say "He is guilty. Crucify Him!" knowing that if He was not crucified, we would have to spend an eternity in hell? As much as we love Jesus, we would have to agree with the Will of our Father. He must die so we can live forever. We would not want to face eternity without His suffering and death in our behalf. From a different motive than the crowd, our directions to Pilate would be the same, "Crucify Him"; but then to Jesus, "I'm sorry you have to die for my sins." The cross shows us the amazing love of God. He did for us what we could not do for ourselves.

Where has all the power gone? The branches are not being filled from the fullness of the Vine, and the sap is being lost through the bruises of sin. Certainly, we do not have to fulfill every item on the check list in order to get to heaven. I cannot, I dare not even try to earn my right to a seat with the saints of God. We get to heaven simply by trusting in Christ alone for our salvation. He has paid the price. All we do is accept His payment in our behalf. However, a greater faith and a greater power by which to live and work can come from entering into a closer relationship with Jesus, the Vine. Let us join in prayer for a return of the power to our lives and to our church that is being experienced by many in the church today and that was experienced by the early Christians. The church can have this power again only as each individual becomes more consistent in using the Gospel, the Word, the

Sacraments, and prayer, and only as we daily repent, believe, and give our lives to Jesus, our Savior and the Lord of the church.

Pray with me the words of a favorite hymn: (TLH 394)

> My faith looks up to Thee,
> Thou Lamb of Calvary, Savior divine.
> Now hear me while I pray;
> Take all my guilt away;
> Oh, let me from this day Be wholly Thine!

> May Thy rich grace impart
> Strength to my fainting heart, My zeal inspire!
> As Thou hast died for me,
> Oh, may my love to Thee
> Pure, warm, and changeless be, A living fire!

> While life's dark maze I tread
> And griefs around me spread, Be Thou my Guide.
> Bid darkness turn to day,
> Wipe sorrow's tears away,
> Nor let me ever stray From Thee aside.

> When ends life's transient dream,
> When death's cold, sullen stream Shall o'er me roll,
> Blest Savior, then, in love,
> Fear and distrust remove;
> Oh, bear me safe above, A ransomed soul! Amen.